War and Conscience in South Africa

War and Conscience in South Africa
The Churches and Conscientious Objection

Catholic Institute for International Relations
and
Pax Christi

First published 1982
CIIR, 22 Coleman Fields, London N1 7AF, UK, and
Pax Christi, St Francis Centre, Pottery Lane, London W11, UK
©1982 Catholic Institute for International Relations and Pax Christi

Catholic Institute for International Relations
    War and conscience in South Africa.
    1. South Africa — Christianity and politics
    I. Title
    261.7   BR115.P7

ISBN 0 904393 73 9

Printed by the Russell Press, Gamble Street, Nottingham, UK.
Design by Jan Brown, 01-837 5296.

Contents

Introduction

When I was still involved in the multiracial student movement in South Africa, a friend of mine, a Christian, who served on my Executive, apologetically excused himself from attending one meeting because he had been called up for military training in the South African Defence Force. He explained that it was as difficult for him as it was for me, as a black person, to carry a *dompas* (reference book). However by 1978 matters on the military front had deteriorated so much that a young white uniformed police constable who was guarding me when I was detained confessed to me the anxiety he and many of his peers felt about serving in the army. He did not think that the racial war in South Africa was one for which he was prepared to lay down his life. By then, following the Angolan military adventure of 1976, the chickens were coming home to roost in the form of countless deaths of young conscripts together with a hasty retreat from foreign soil. It appears that the Angolan war opened the eyes of many decent white people to the dangers of fighting in a war that did not seem to have any moral basis. Granted that, then, it was very sad to receive a letter from the present Bishop of St John's, Transkei, admitting support for his sons who felt it their duty to their country to fight in the SADF. I don't think that it is being too uncharitable to suggest that the bishop could only have arrived at that conclusion if he had taken off his theological cap and donned that of a white South African. Is that morally defensible?

This book is evidence of a moral reflection among young white people in South Africa called, against their will, to fight in the SADF. A large number of them raise questions not so much about the fact of war, generally, although some do, as about the moral basis of this particular war. They are clearly entitled to do so if they are to put their lives at risk and, even more, if they are to be expected to take the life of another.

7

The question that has not been raised sufficiently in this debate is whether the war and preparations for war can be justified on the basis of the just war principle? Does that principle apply to wars directed at the citizens of a country — something akin to a civil war? Can it be applied if the state has no moral authority to govern? In Namibia, for example, and by international law, South Africa has no authority or legal status. Can the will of an illegal invader or an occupying country be enforced by legal means? In South Africa, itself, by what right can the present Nationalist regime claim moral legitimacy over the lives of the vast majority of black people who cannot elect a government or, by constitutional means, seek to influence the political affairs of the country?

It is my view, that these questions would remain, even if the government was just and benevolent. However, the fact of the matter in South Africa is that the regime is notoriously corrupt inasmuch as in its political philosophy and the brutal suppression of legitimate dissent, it upholds immoral values. Christianity is founded on the moral imperative of love. In I John 2.9 we read that 'whoever says that he is in the light, yet hates his brother, is in the darkness to this very hour'. It is not enough for a Christian to recite 'Give unto Caesar . . .' or Romans 13. The prior issue is the fact that all things belong to God: 'The earth is the Lord's and everything that's in it'. Human beings are stewards, to discharge God's tasks on his behalf. The exercise of the authority and dominion still has to bear the mark of God's love. On the basis of this Christians uphold the positive moral presumptions: equality of persons in God; the unity of the human family in God; the value of individual life and the goodness of created existence. On all these counts the South African regime is morally indefensible and, if so, then no Christian need take up arms to defend it. In fact, I can go as far as to say that no Christian should defend it.

A more difficult matter, however, would be what one should do, or how far can one go in resisting the coercive power of the regime? Perhaps the words of a survivor of the Auschwitz holocaust are pertinent: 'It is evil to assent actively or passively to evil as an instrument, as its observer or as its victim . . .'. That is Jewish religion. Christianity teaches that when one is faced with a difficult choice between two evils, one is bound to choose the one which will result in minimum harm or suffering. It is our conscience, the judgment of practical reason, that guides us as to what we ought to do. In Christianity one does have a duty to obey one's conscience. The corollary to that is the fact that we accept responsibility for our actions taken in a true conscience. The moral decisions taken according to our conscience are informed by our Christian moral and social teaching. In the exercise of one's conscience one asserts one's freedom.

I think many black people may dismiss the question of conscientious objection as a matter of irrelevance to them. That would be a costly mistake. Apart from anything else we can see that, especially in the homelands, blacks are being deployed in military service. Sooner or later this will no longer be voluntary but compulsory conscription. We have seen it happen already in Namibia. When that happens the tragedy of it all will become intensified. What about an encounter of fellow-oppressed on either side of the firing line? The divisions within families will be enormous. The moral issues debated today demand the participation of black people as well.

For a different reason black people have an interest in the matter. It will help us to clarify our minds about our responsibility and commitment to the cause of liberation. Surely a debate on moral responsibility in one part of the life of the country must raise the same issues in other spheres of political life. This also gives an opportunity for many white people to redeem themselves from the judgement of their being part of the problem and to transform themselves into effective agents for change. Selective objection constitutes just such a disavowal of the oppressive system.

What about the response of the churches? Clearly the leadership of the South African Council of Churches is commendable. The denominations, however, still have to make a clearer statement of commitment on the whole issue. Now that the World Reformed Alliance has unequivocally declared apartheid a heresy, then the churches in South Africa should be able to exercise more discipline over their clergy who serve in the SADF. An even more consistent line would be to withdraw chaplaincy services to the SADF in its present form and arrange for the pastoral care of men with the parishes where the army camps are based. It is just not good enough for the church to say, as the Provincial Synod of the Church of the Province of South Africa did in 1978, that it supports those who feel called to defend South Africa on both sides of the border. That is equivocating. It must be obvious that a commitment to provide ministry and pastoral care to those who are dying for freedom must entail a withdrawal of similar care within the context and structures of the SADF. Those who fight for freedom need to feel that they can trust the church to act according to its commitment. Verbal protests and statements of support are not enough. Jesus was not a detached supporter of the poor and the oppressed. He took steps to free them and to give them hope. He suffered with them and denounced the rich and the powerful (Mk 10.23).

There is, however, hope when the church becomes Christian.

9

When it upholds and lives by the teachings of Jesus Christ, seeking, with integrity, to respond to the commandment of love in the knowledge of guilt and in the hope of forgiveness. The church is committed to work, in the ultimate, for the reconciliation of man with God through Christ and for the final realisation of God's purposes. The penultimate, however, is the world of imperfect man, as Bonhoeffer would say. We dare not assume perfection; but we hold the hope that God has called us to a new condition of life and we guide society towards the attainment of these goals.

War and Conscience in South Africa is a contribution to the debate by young South Africans intimately involved with the issues here outlined. For people grappling with these problems inside South Africa, it provides an account of the growth of the war resistance movement which enables them to see it in the context of the broader struggle for the liberation of South Africa. It also enables the Christians of the world to see for themselves that the cause of the war resisters involves principles which lie at the heart not only of Christianity but also of any genuine humanism. The book also documents the worsening tragedy of a South Africa in which these principles of conscience can no longer be upheld within the framework of the law. To the western countries which are the economic and diplomatic backers of the South African regime in the international community it is an urgent appeal to examine the values they are really defending in South Africa. The authors and CIIR and Pax Christi, the publishers, are to be commended for such a lucid presentation, objective and faithfully documented. This is no propaganda tract. Read on!

Nyameko Pityana
Woughton, Milton Keynes
December 1982

1. The Militarisation of South Africa

The Churches and the Apartheid System

The opposition of all the Christian denominations except the Dutch Reformed to the National Party's Republic Day celebrations in 1981 highlighted a process that had accelerated rapidly during the late 1970s, a growing rift between church and state in South Africa, widened in large measure by the churches' position on conscientious objection. The white Dutch Reformed churches, which have 2.6 million members, or 60% of white Christians, supported the celebrations. The Christian protests against Republic Day symbolised for South Africa's minority government a major public denial by the churches that the National Party and the Afrikaner-dominated state represented more than the sectional interests of some whites. If there was a 'Christian nation', as Dr Malan had supposed when the National Party came to power in 1948, the protests suggested that it was not embodied in the white minority that ruled South Africa.

This Christian denial not only of apartheid society but also, implicitly, of the very legitimacy of South Africa's government, came at the climax of several decades of liberal opposition by the churches to racial discrimination and white minority rule. It is in this context that the churches' teaching on military service and relations between churches and the military in South Africa must be set. It gives the important issues of pacifism, conscientious objection and theories of the just war an immediacy for South African Christians not perhaps found in European countries, and an international significance in the struggle against apartheid. For young white South Africans such issues can become part of a life crisis that begins when call-up papers arrive. For this reason it is helpful to begin with a brief historical account of the church-state conflict that forms a background to the debate about military service.

The roots of church-state conflict

By the early part of this century the imported religion of Christianity, after over a century of missionary endeavour, was taking on a definite South African character. Black Christians now had three religious alternatives. They might join the multiracial denominations that, on the whole, stemmed from the British Isles with white culture, liturgy and leadership. Or they could join the all-black mission churches, also under white leadership and answerable ultimately — with the exception of the Dutch Reformed — to mission boards in North America and Europe. Finally they could repudiate white paternalism and control by seeking African expressions of Christianity in the independent churches whose two great branches have been labelled as Ethiopian and Zionist.

The white church, linked by money and personnel to Europe in varying degrees, came to reflect the diversity of its members. The largest denomination, the powerful Nederduitse Gereformeerde Kerk (NGK — the 'Dutch Reformed'), and some of its splinter churches, differed from the rest in having headquarters and mission thrust primarily in South Africa. It gave rise to an 'African NGK', an 'Indian Reformed Church' and a 'Coloured Sendingkerk', daughter churches under the umbrella of the parent white church. These churches were later to play an important role in formulating a black theology which radically challenged the apartheid system, and finally separated entirely from the white NGK. The NGK became swept up in, and provided religious motifs within, the tide of Afrikaner nationalism. Its nationalist theology conveniently obscured the differences in interests between Afrikaner workers, farmers and businessmen. On the other hand, the rest of the 'white' church played a minor but important role in the life of the English-speaking community.

The English-speaking churches also consolidated white privilege. However, the ideology of Afrikaner nationalism that found its roots in NGK themes of Christian nationalism and the separation of the races enabled the English-speaking churches to contrast themselves as 'liberal'. But this liberalism was not entirely toothless. The report by Archbishop Geoffrey Clayton of Cape Town on 'The Church and the Nation' was a strong and progressive Anglican statement on reform issued at the end of the Second World War. It recommended not only a wide extension of the franchise to blacks but recognition of the African Mineworkers Union. In 1948, the Catholic Bishop of Cape Town, Monsignor Henneman, described apartheid as 'noxious, un-Christian and destructive'. Men like Trevor Huddleston and Michael Scott, the latter going to jail for three months during his Campaign for Right and Justice, moved far beyond official gradualism into a more radical form of liberalism.

Social justice

However little impact the strand of liberalism in the English-speaking churches made on South African society, it created the religious culture from which black Christians drew their own political themes. James Calata, an Anglican minister who was secretary-general of the African National Congress between 1936 and 1949, saw Christ as 'the champion of freedom'. From the same soil came Albert Luthuli. After a decade of National Party rule which had wrested control of schools from most of the churches — the Catholics clung on at great financial cost and at a price in dependence on white support — the liberalism of some churchmen was sharpened. At the 1960 Cottesloe conference it began to infect some prominent members of the NGK, now shaken by the human cost of apartheid in top gear. The formation of the Christian Institute in 1963 symbolised the reality of a small but significant group of white Christians in South Africa who now saw the struggle against apartheid as a constitutive part of Christian witness and evangelisation.

There had been eighteen black participants amongst a large gathering at Cottesloe, including Professor Z.K. Matthews and Bishop Alphaeus Zulu. By the end of the 1960s, as the wave of independence swept over the European colonies in Africa, the black majority in all the denominations were listened to with a new attention. The degree to which they were heeded varied considerably from church to church. In the NGK with its white majority, the head of the daughter Sendingkerk, Dr Allan Boesak, later became an international figure as world moderator of the Reformed Churches and renowned theologian. He was effectively rejected by the white parent NGK. A black theology developed and the philosophy of black consciousness asserted the dignity and independence of blacks in the face of white liberal paternalism. The message given to the churches was that change came not from pious appeals to the privileged, but through community organising, trades unions, student political organisation, and studied strategies of protest. This message was reinforced in the turbulent history of the 1970s.

After post-war verbal condemnations of apartheid by the churches, the voice of the oppressed in the last decade has increasingly spoken of 'resistance' and called the churches to resist apartheid actively. The white church hierarchies have slowly, and sometimes reluctantly, made this voice their own. In February 1972 in a 'Call to Conscience' supported by the Catholic hierarchy, the Catholic Church firmly denounced the injustices of the South African system and

13

committed itself to the anti-apartheid struggle. In further commitments in 1977 they spoke with a radical voice of support for liberation in a document of great critical authority. Meanwhile the issue of conscientious objection had, in the wake of the 1974 coup in Portugal with its ramifications in southern Africa, set churches and state on collision course.

The voice of the oppressed

The hierarchical structures of the white-led churches have come under strong pressure to adapt to the new reality of black Christianity, a faith shaped by a daily existence under oppression. The change has been manifested in the rapid rise in the number of black ministers and the appearance of blacks in key positions of church leadership and government. The change from white to black leadership has been most rapid in those churches with short training for the ministry, so that leadership positions in the Catholic Church, with its additional compulsory celibacy, are still 80% in white hands. This contrasts sharply with the South African Council of Churches which represents the majority of the Protestant denominations in South Africa and has produced outstanding black leaders of international renown like Bishop Desmond Tutu. Not surprisingly it was the independent Christian Institute and the SACC which bore the brunt of Christian participation in the struggle for social justice in the 1970s, and the resulting wrath and harassment of the government.

But it would be a form of inverse racialism to believe that 'Africanising' the leadership necessarily involves the churches in a radical commitment to social justice. The ministerial role, inherited from the relatively privileged life-style of white pastors and priests, has no inbuilt guarantees that its incumbent will not become a servant of the status quo. Authoritarian responses to those struggling for change amongst the poor are not limited to white church leaders. Nonetheless the different black church leaders in South Africa have in common the humiliating lack of political and human rights experienced by all blacks. From a black pulpit the view of the apartheid state and its armed forces is likely to be different from that from a white.

What all churches also share is the fundamental problem that Christian insights about, and action in relation to, social justice have largely in the past been expressed *outside* church structures. The strong Christian presence in the African National Congress, in youth movements and women's movements, has shown how few outlets the churches supply for lay leadership in ecclesial structures. The problem of translating verbal commitments to oppose apartheid and work for social justice into action has to greater or lesser extents bedevilled all churches. At the root of this failure has been an institutional inability to create relevant new structures, basic communities, movements of committed Christians, and to give them a priority greater than that of the parish. On the other hand, groups like the Catholic Defence League and Christian League, right-wing white minority groups covertly funded by the South African government and officially repudiated by the Catholic and Methodist churches respectively, have had an influence disproportionate to their numbers.

Four key issues for white Christians

The voice of the poor in the churches in South Africa has been instrumental only indirectly in stimulating the debate about conscientious objection. Except in Namibia, blacks are not called up for military service, though poverty and unemployment drive many to join the Bantustan armies which are an important structural part of the South African armed forces. The Ciskei regime has also in force a Defence Bill which makes military training compulsory for all Ciskei 'citizens' between 18 and 65. In bringing this issue to the fore white radicals, both outside and inside the churches, have taken the lead. The issue is essentially one for whites and its growing importance illustrates the dialogue going on between white and black Christians. It is primarily in the climate of non-racial co-operation in the struggle for justice that the issue of the churches' relationship to apartheid's military apparatus has grown into a central concern for South African Christians. This relationship at present hinges on the attitudes of church and state to four key issues:

1. the growing militarisation of South African society
2. conscientious objection to military service (or as it is more commonly referred to outside South Africa, 'war resistance')
3. the question of military chaplaincies, their existence and role
4. the increasing mass resistance to apartheid and the escalating guerrilla war of the liberation movements.

The urgency of all four issues has become more acute with the SADF occupation of Namibia and southern Angola employing up to 100,000 troops, the army increasingly being deployed in South Africa itself to combat mass resistance and ANC military activity, which increased 200% in 1981.

Militarisation and 'National Security'

After 1960 and the international reaction to the Sharpeville massacre, particularly from the newly independent African states, Pretoria embarked on military expansion. The end-point was to be the most

15

powerful and sophisticated military machine on the African continent and in the southern hemisphere. From R40 million for 1959/1960 the defence budget increased to R2,900 million for 1982/1983.[1] Universal conscription for white male citizens was introduced in 1967.

By 1972 the initial period of national service had been raised from nine to 12 months, followed by 19 days' service annually for five years. At the end of 1975 national servicemen who had completed their initial training began to be called up for three-month tours of active service, as Mozambique and Angola moved into independence under radical governments. In 1977 the initial period of national service was increased to two years, followed by one 30-day camp each year for eight years. The three-month call-ups, originally needed to meet the manpower needs of the South African invasion of Angola, have been retained. The estimated total manpower of the South African Defence Force (SADF) increased from 78,000 in 1960 to 494,000 in 1979. Its standing operational force increased over the same period from 11,500 to 180,000.[2] During the course of 1982, legislation was introduced extending the periods of service after two years' training to 720 days spread over 12 years. Older men would also be required to perform military duties.

Just as Sharpeville had heralded the first wave of military expansion, transforming a modest, almost colonial army into a technologically proficient military machine, so the urban risings of 1976 heralded a new and more profound militarisation of society. Where once there had been frequent ritual warnings to civil society to brace up for attacks from the forces of international communism, in 1977 the concept of 'total strategy' was broadcast. It marked a campaign to militarise an entire society and brought to prominence the ideology of national security that had been largely fostered in the United States' military academies for export to the Third World. The philosophy of national security defines the quest for social justice in countries marked by gross disparities in wealth and ruled by oppressive, authoritarian regimes, as a struggle between 'Christian civilisation' and 'communism'. It lends itself easily to the National Party's claim to embody Christian nationalism by defining all opponents as subversive communists set on undermining a rationally ordered, biblically founded, Christian society.

Apartheid: the changing form of repression

The South African state, with its massive proliferation of an

---

1. International Defence and Aid Fund (IDAF), *The Apartheid War Machine*, London, April 1980, table 1, p.10.
2. IDAF, *op.cit.*, table VII, p.41.

Afrikaner bureaucracy, enshrined a principle of arbitrary authoritarianism. This principle was codified in over 300 separate laws controlling the movement of blacks and regulating their relationship to the white controlled economy. As apartheid laws proliferated, blacks were taught to become subordinate to faceless institutional controls and to accept their role within the system as movable labour units.

But blacks soon demonstrated their capacity to transcend their allotted roles, and the state moved to expand the role of the military as its principal instrument for maintaining authoritarian patterns and institutional controls. The major moves towards the militarisation of society were thus essentially a reaction to failures of bureaucratic methods of control. It might be argued that in new industrialising societies, in which workers are able to organise within the framework of technologically complex industries, this failure is inevitable. Conservative bureaucracies will be outwitted and overwhelmed as resistance to the state from articulate and skilled workers and intellectuals grows. This process will be accompanied by big business and transnationals seeking escape from state controls and chafing at bureaucratic constraint on private enterprise, though willing whenever necessary to use the state's military power to repress workers.

The particular path of industrial development in South Africa thus required growing military intervention in society as it did in Latin America. Compared to bureaucratic controls — but only compared to them — the institutional subordination required in military life was 'modernising'. It required a move away from traditional patterns. The ideology of national security was shared by a new breed of technocrats, masters of complex military hardware and computer printouts. Their natural partners were the technocratic masters of modern industry. Their natural world was the international arena of arms sales, defence academies, and global 'strategy', not the atavistic, national domain of Afrikaner bureaucrats.

If the horizon of the South African bureaucracy was harsh control of blacks as labour units, that of the 'modernising' military was frighteningly more grandiose: control over all aspects of society, across borders, into hearts and minds. This totalitarian vision was justified by the belief that South Africa was suffering from a 'total onslaught' which required a total response. The premise of 'total strategy' was described by the then chief of the SADF, General Magnus Malan, in 1977. 'South Africa is today . . . involved in total war. The war is not only an area for the soldier. Everyone is involved and has a role to play.'[3] According to a statement by the then Officer

---

3. *The Star*, Johannesburg, 10 September 1977.

Commanding Natal Command, Brigadier C.J. Lloyd (now Major-General Lloyd, in charge of operations in Namibia) two years later, this total involvement was required because: 'Enemy actions are directed against the Republic of South Africa in the political, economic, psychological and security fields. On its part, the Republic of South Africa has to act or counteract in all these fields.'[4] He believed that in 1979 80% of defensive action would be essentially non-military though supported by military personnel.[5]

Thus national security was a doctrine that found a place for the humblest citizen, summoning him or her to join in the battle against a titanic and pervasive, though ill-defined, evil called communism. For whites, and a minority of blacks, in the face of 'white Moscow communists in Maputo sending secret legions bent on destruction', the only response was obedience to authority. The possible goal, as in Namibia, was the co-option and conscription of blacks, attainable only in the improbable event of their accepting the state's doctrine of national security in a racially divided society.

The national security ideology finally became official state policy with the appointment of the then Minister of Defence, Mr P.W. Botha, as Prime Minister in October 1978. The appointment of this ally of General Magnus Malan set in train what amounted to a creeping military coup. By streamlining government through a reduction in the number of civil service departments, P.W. Botha began to trim the powerful Afrikaner bureaucracy. In February 1982, he eased out its natural leader, Dr Andries Treurnicht, and gained control of the bureaucrat-dominated Transvaal Party. National planning became concentrated in the State Security Council (SSC) with the downgrading of the cabinet. The Deputy Minister of Defence was moved to become Minister of Justice, while General Magnus Malan was made Minister of Defence, taking over the portfolio from the Prime Minister. Military men served on interdepartmental policy planning committees. The National Party in parliament increasingly used the institution to broadcast policy, simply ignoring opposition protest, and finding itself pitted against an increasingly powerful splinter Conservative Party rallying in the Transvaal around Dr Treurnicht. This was to be countered in 1983 by the creation of an Executive Presidency with a seven year term and no machinery for impeachment.

---

4. Brigadier C.J. Lloyd, *The Importance of Rural Development in the Defence Strategy of South Africa and the Need for Private Sector Involvement*, paper delivered to a workshop of the Natal Region of the Urban Foundation, Durban, 10 August 1979, p.3.
5. ibid., p.10.

A military society

Once in control of key state apparatus, the military have moved rapidly to implement their policies. 'Key points' legislation has defined large sections of modern industry as central to total strategy; industrial managements are required to offer adequate security protection to all such installations. Troops now appear in conjunction with police at riots, on raids, and routine road checks. Soldiers teach in black schools, collect taxes and work in medical and agricultural programmes, 'winning the hearts and minds'. Large advertisements ask drivers to pick up troops travelling home on leave while Barclays Bank specifically advertises for military customers. Press, radio and television feature 'friendly chats' from military experts who play a growing part in directing news and preparing the public for major military actions against neighbouring countries. The great parastatal armaments manufacturer ARMSCOR draws in numerous subsidiary enterprises to the growing sector involved with military production. In schools, Youth Preparedness and cadet courses, military qualities are stressed and the mystique of bush warfare extolled, a tradition underpinned in history classes by the glorification of Boer guerrilla tactics in the Anglo-Boer war.

Military service in any country requires a suspension of critical judgment and subordination of individuals to rapid responses to commands from authority. In South Africa these patterns are not only imposed by conscription but annually reinforced in camps and glorified in the mass media. A growing number of young people, unwilling to subject themselves to processes they find dehumanising, but obliged to do so by conscription, have suffered nervous breakdowns and been sent for psychiatric treatment. This severe pressure on individuals seems likely to increase as militarisation is presented as the central formative experience for South Africans, defining them as 'normal' or 'traitors'. It is evident that mindless obedience and uncritical acceptance of authority's myths are necessary qualities for the survival of ruling minorities in undemocratic divided societies. For this reason it is not surprising that *all* the white political parties are united in their strident opposition to selective conscientious objection. None have dared to demythologise the Afrikaner and ruling white definition of 'patriotism'.

The Churches' Response to Militarisation

The scope and extent of the militarisation of South African society has taken the churches by surprise and found them ill-prepared to mount an effective campaign against it. This is partly because national security has become the dominant political philosophy of the state and practical opposition to it would be perceived by traditional western churchmen as 'political'. But it is also because the advocacy of conscientious objection takes the churches outside the law in South Africa and makes individual churchmen susceptible to prosecution and imprisonment. The churches have therefore rarely moved beyond moral considerations of the rights of individuals to conscientious objector status, arguments about military chaplains and broad statements about violence.

Most of the major denominations do not hold a pacifist position nor do they demand a pacifist approach from their members. Yet nearly all their leaders urge the use of peaceful methods of change and have shown a growing willingness to denounce the use of violence to maintain the status quo. The SACC has a commission studying issues of violence and non-violence which has been very active in propagating attitudes of non-violent protest and the views of pacifist conscientious objectors.

The churches have rarely gone further than this, to active corporate war resistance. Nevertheless there have been striking instances when churches and individual church leaders have explicitly linked the individual issues of conscientious objection and violence to the broader social question of the injustice of apartheid society. Already in 1974, the Catholic Archbishop of Durban, Denis Hurley, warned:

> In my view any conflict arising in the near future on our borders will be in the nature of civil conflict, with people of the same country fighting each other. I believe it is our duty to discourage people from getting involved in this military conflict because of the realities of the South African situation — a situation of oppression . . . We must recognise the right of liberation movements to react to the situation in this country. We must look for a peaceful resolution to the question and face it with Christian conscience.[6]

In January 1979 Bill Burnett, the Anglican Archbishop of Cape Town and then head of the local Anglican Church (Church of the Province of South Africa, CPSA), warned that unless whites 'transmute' the root of apartheid for a more equitable feeding of the branches of the state '. . . this will be a time of killing'. In the face of this dreadful possibility the role of Christians would be likely to vary. Some, he believed, would try to transform apartheid by organising

---

6. Quoted in *Church and Conscience:* A Collection of Church and Other Statements on Conscientious Objection in South Africa, Christian Citizenship Department of the Methodist Church of Southern Africa, 1980, p.16.

pressure for change in its social structures and some would seek to achieve this end through the written word. Still other Christians might conclude that all peaceful means to achieve change had been tried. He continued that since passive resistance was virtually impossible in South Africa, they might well then decide, as some already had, that they should join guerrilla movements 'beyond South Africa's borders'.[7]

These acknowledgements by white churchmen of the possible legitimacy of armed struggle were followed by open repudiation of National Security philosophy by black churchmen. In October 1980 SACC Secretary-General Bishop Desmond Tuto made it unmistakeably clear that black South Africans were 'totally unconcerned about some external threat, even if it be true that the communists are hungry for South Africa . . . They are concerned about the present stark reality, which is their oppression as victims of injustice and exploitation under the most vicious system since nazism.' His conclusion was that blacks did not, anyway, consider the country as it was presently ordered to be defensible.[8] At almost the same moment the Council of Churches in Namibia was writing to the State President of South Africa pleading with him to drop legislation bringing into effect compulsory conscription in Namibia for blacks. The argument of the Church leaders was that the conflict in Namibia would thus be rapidly transformed into a civil war.

In the last two years the churches have been confronted with the first concrete results of South Africa's militarisation: a massive rise in extra-territorial action by the SADF. The dynamic of vast military growth has proved to be military adventures involving large numbers of troops, or trained surrogates, in Angola and Mozambique, and to a lesser extent in Zambia and Zimbabwe, pursuing policies of destabilisation. That these actions are arguably contrary to the interests of South Africa's white minority indicates the degree to which military logic has taken over the conduct of national affairs.

The militarisation of South Africa therefore sets the churches a challenge at a number of different levels. Its purpose is to sustain apartheid in a modernised form and to extend South Africa's control throughout southern Africa. Its technique is to instil in civil society an unthinking obedience to the repressive institutions of the white minority and an uncritical acceptance of state propaganda. Its propaganda target is society as a whole, and in particular, the potential number of young whites whose idealism might draw them towards a quest for a non-racial and democratic South Africa. Its

7. *The Argus*, Cape Town, 31 January 1979.
8. *The Star*, 16 October 1980.

result is to promulgate a definition of 'Christian civilisation' whose heretical nature threatens the integrity of the Christian churches and whose unconditional demand for loyalty directly challenges their fidelity to the gospel.

2. Military Service and War Resistance

Black Christians now represent 75-80% of the membership of South Africa's churches, roughly commensurate with the ratio of blacks to whites in society as a whole. Their growing importance as the vast majority of Christians has meant that their perceptions of the South African Defence Force have become more widely accepted in the churches. During the mid-1970s their message that the SADF was used to fight black workers, students and political organisations rather than to defend the majority of the population was graphically illustrated. The wide military roads built around black townships and the SADF garrisons at their periphery demonstrated a form of internal colonialism.

The worker unrest and student revolt of the 1970s evoked from the South African state ruthless forms of repression unacceptable to even the most blinkered churchmen. As growing church-state conflict corresponded with the new programme of militarisation, it was not surprising that the issue of resistance to military service began to pre-occupy the churches. As the number of war resisters grew, resistance began to play an important part in the spectrum of contentious issues fuelling church-state clashes. However, the growth in the practice of war resistance, rather than discussion about it, was a slow process that took until the 1980s to cause serious concern to the South African authorities.

Conscription and Initial Resistance

The legal foundations of military service are to be found in the Defence Act of 1957,[1] which still serves as the basis for the structure of the apartheid war machine and service in it. In 1961, after extensive

---

1. No.44 of 1957.

internal unrest had prompted the declaration of a state of emergency and the mobilisation of the army, and when the National Party regime was confronted with unprecedented international hostility, the period of compulsory military service was increased from three to nine months. In introducing the new legislation the then Minister of Defence, J.J. Fouché, called on white mothers to 'give up their sons in defence of their land'.[2]

At first there was an intake of 7,000 men into the Citizen Force.[3] This was soon extended and by 1964 there was an annual intake of about 16,500.[4] With the country's growing international isolation, the replacement of Fouché by P.W. Botha as Minister of Defence in 1965 and the election to the premiership of former Justice Minister B.J. Vorster the following year, greater emphasis was given to the build-up of the armed forces. In 1967 the government introduced universal conscription for all white male South African citizens and certain categories of non-citizens. The government was now embarked on full preparations to meet the threat of the southern African liberation movements which had begun armed struggles in Angola in 1961, Mozambique in 1964, Namibia in 1966 and Zimbabwe in 1967, and had conducted a limited number of sabotage actions in South Africa itself.

In terms of the 1967 amendment *all* national servicemen were required to render service of nine months; for the previous six years individuals had been chosen by ballot for service. No provision was made for conscientious objectors. However, there were two ways in which a certain limited category of objectors could be afforded relief by administrative action; allotment or exemption. In both cases the relief provided went no further than the posting of some of these objectors to positions where they could render military service in a non-combatant capacity.

Lawful non-combatant status

a. *Allotment:* Section 67 (3) of the Defence Act provides that:

> The registering officer shall as far as may be practicable allot any person who to his knowledge bona fide belongs and adheres to a recognised religious denomination by the tenets whereof its members may not participate in war, to a unit where such person will be able to render service in the defence of the Republic in a non-combatant capacity.

---

2. *Hansard:* House of Assembly Debates, 18 May 1961, col. 7005-7. Fouché later became State President.
3. The branch of the SADF in which most conscripts are placed for their initial service. It makes up the bulk of the SADF.
4. See James Barber, *South Africa's Foreign Policy 1945-1970*, London, 1973, 190-201 for a useful account of the early years of South Africa's military expansion.

This section merely creates the possibility for a conscientious objector to be assigned to non-combatant service subject to administrative discretion. This is not a right which one can insist on in a court of law. The registering officer may exercise his discretion only when the objector is a member of a recognised religious denomination 'by the tenets whereof its members may not participate in war'. In practice this means today members of recognised religious pacifist groups, such as the Society of Friends, Jehovah's Witnesses, Seventh Day Adventists and other small groups who gained this 'concession' as 'peace churches'. It is church membership and not conscientious objection which forms the basis or criterion for such administrative action. Moreover, the denominations catered for under this section form a minute part of the Christian community in South Africa.

Conscientious objectors provided for under this section need not be posted to non-combatant units. They can and have been posted to combatant units where they have been required to render military service but in a non-combatant capacity, for example, as cooks or clerks. In practice it is not the registering officer, but the commanding officer of the unit concerned, who assigns such persons to non-combatant duties. And in this respect each unit is a law unto itself. In some units the objector is excused from military drill, while in others he is even required to march and perform rifle drill with a broomstick or metal tubing, or a small tree trunk, as a substitute rifle.

b. *Exemption:* Conscientious objectors may also be granted exemption from combatant service in the SADF under section 97 (3), which provides that:

> a person who bona fide belongs and adheres to a recognised religious denomination by the tenets whereof its members may not participate in war, may be granted exemption from serving in any combatant capacity, but shall, if called upon to do so, serve in a non-combatant capacity.

Exemptions are granted by the exemption board. Again, the power to grant such exemption is purely discretionary, does not employ conscientious objection as a criterion, and where the exemption is granted it is only partial.

Unlawful conscientious objection

In terms of the 1967 legislation any person who refused to render military service without just cause, when called up to do so, committed an offence and was liable to imprisonment of up to three months which might be repeated upon each unlawful refusal until the offender was no longer liable to render military service. Conscientious objection was not considered to be a just cause. A person who was

25

charged under this legislation was tried initially in a civilian magistrate's court and if found guilty, was usually sentenced to 90 days in military Detention Barracks.

In Detention Barracks the conscientious objector, along with the other inmates, was subject to the Detention Barracks Regulations and the usual military discipline.[5] Failure to comply with these regulations or lawful commands rendered an offender liable to a variety of punishments, including solitary confinement for a period of up to 14 days, with or without spare diet (bread and water). Such punishment could be repeated for each act of disobedience until termination of the original sentence of imprisonment.

Initial resistance

The first incidents of war resistance had already occurred under the ballot system and the introduction of universal conscription in 1967 prompted an increase in the number of such incidents. Some objectors stood trial and were imprisoned while others, usually the more politically motivated, left the country. Yet the total number of war resisters remained small.

Nevertheless, this was an important period as it marked the beginning of major clashes between church and state on the conscientious objection issue, although only a very small and relatively marginal section of the church was involved. By far the majority of conscientious objectors who were imprisoned were Jehovah's Witnesses, who refused to recognise all state authorities indiscriminately. They were thrown into Detention Barracks and on completion of their terms of imprisonment, were again called up to render military service. This process was repeated again and again so that some Witnesses served up to four years or more in Detention Barracks. But despite this virtual persecution a growing number of Witnesses continued to resist military service.

Within Detention Barracks the Witnesses refused to wear the regulation military dress and to perform military drill, and as a result suffered. Their civilian clothes were removed and they were not issued with clothing other than the military uniform. One Witness, who served three terms in Detention Barracks, mentioned that he spent the winter months in nothing but his underclothes.[6] In addition, the Witnesses were punished for their refusal. Many were sentenced to repeated periods in solitary confinement. When the Witnesses

---

5. The Detention Barracks Regulations were promulgated as Government Notice R1190 on 8 December 1961 (*Government Gazette Extraordinary*, No.48).
6. Etienne Mureinik, 'Conscientious Objection: The United States and South Africa' (1976), in *Lexis*, Cape Town, NUSAS, 1978.

26

appealed to the courts, this form of persecution was sanctioned by no less a body than the Appeal Court.[7] The Jehovah's Witnesses protested vigorously against this inhumane treatment of persons whose only crime was to be true to their convictions, but for some years nothing was done.

Accommodation of the initial resistance

In 1972 the length of compulsory service was increased to an initial period of 12 months, followed by 19 days' service annually for five years. Simultaneously the sentence for unlawful conscientious objectors and others unlawfully refusing to render military service was increased to a maximum of 15 months' imprisonment (under section 126A), but with a provision which marked the state's attempt to accommodate resistance from the Jehovah's Witnesses. These provisions were designed only to eliminate embarrassing opposition without undermining the compulsory service system. They stipulated that anyone who had been sentenced to Detention Barracks under this section and for a period of 12 months or more, could not be sentenced again. In practice offenders were sentenced to the maximum period but the last three months have almost always been remitted. Thus, from 1972 most offenders served only 12 months in Detention Barracks.

Within Detention Barracks the authorities also tried to appease the Jehovah's Witnesses. They were issued with blue 'conscientious objector' overalls, were segregated from the other inmates and were excused from military drill. The Jehovah's Witnesses still enjoy this privileged status in Detention Barracks which they gained through weight of numbers and by refusal to compromise.

Development of the Conflict

However, subsequent events were to show that the conflict between church and state on the issue of war resistance was just beginning. In the early 1970s the revival of internal extra-parliamentary opposition and the intensification of the wars of liberation in the neighbouring states contributed to an increase in the number of war resisters of other categories, including members of the major denominations. The latter were thereby induced to focus on the problem.

The 1974 SACC resolution

Against the background of the collapse of the Portuguese government

---

7. In S v *Schoeman; S v Martin en Andere*, 1971 (4) SA 248 (AD).

under the weight of its colonial wars, the annual conference of the SACC gathered at Hammanskraal on 31 July 1974 under the motto 'Daring to Live for Christ'. The conference opened with a lively debate on the role of the church in South Africa. During this debate Rev. Douglas Bax, a Presbyterian minister, stood up and, in a challenging statement, remarked 'neither the churches nor the SACC had been in the lead of doing something practical to change the status quo in South Africa. Isn't it time for us to consider seriously whether the SACC should challenge young men on the score of conscientious objection?'[8]

The following day he placed a motion on conscientious objection and military chaplains before the conference, maintaining that this was the only thing the church could do rather than just talk. 'There is no time left,' he said. 'This motion is an attempt to dare to live for Christ.'[9] The motion provoked a storm at the conference and there was an attempt to have it dropped, but Christian Institute leader Dr Beyers Naude argued that the situation of violence was escalating and the SACC should not delay any longer: 'we have all been agonising about problems raised in this motion, and thus none of us has come to this subject unprepared. To wait for another year for the next SACC conference would be too long, since the situation of violence is going to escalate.'[10]

The motion was finally discussed on the third day, voted on clause by clause and passed with a few amendments. The final resolution was passed unanimously. Below are the key parts of the text of this resolution which is given in its entirety in Appendix A.

> In the light of this the Conference:
> reminds its member churches that both Catholic and Reformation theology has regarded the taking up of arms as justifiable, if at all, only in order to fight a 'just war';
> points out that the theological definition of a 'just war' excludes war in defence of a basically unjust and discriminatory society;
> points out that the Republic of South Africa is at present a fundamentally unjust and discriminatory society and that this injustice and discrimination constitutes the primary, institutionalised violence which has provoked the counter-violence of the terrorists or freedom fighters;
> points out that the military forces of our country are being prepared to defend this unjust and discriminatory society and that the

---

8. *EcuNews Bulletin* (hereinafter referred to as *EcuNews*), Johannesburg, SACC, 5 August 1974.
9. ibid.
10. ibid.

threat of military force is in fact already used to defend the status quo against moves for radical change from outside the white electorate;

maintains that it is hypocritical to deplore the violence of terrorists or freedom fighters while we ourselves prepare to defend our society with its primary, institutionalised violence by means of yet more violence; . . .

questions the basis upon which chaplains are seconded to the military forces lest their presence indicate moral support for the defence of our unjust and discriminatory society.

In the SACC statement the issue of individual moral decision was set firmly in the context of the justice of the cause to be fought for. It was the particular context of apartheid rather than the general principle of pacifism that informed the teaching. Conscientious objection followed not from a pre-determined refusal to bear arms but from an analysis of the purpose and consequences of bearing arms in South Africa. This was anathema to government.

By invoking the 'just war' theme with its essentially social calculus — (originating at a time when the church hoped to regulate as a majority religion the life of the *corpus christianum*)— the SACC was courting violent reaction. The previous issues of conscientious objection with the Jehovah's Witnesses focused on the rights of individuals to oppose all wars on grounds of conscience. It was answered by accommodating individuals within the military system. The SACC statement, on the other hand, spoke not so much about individual rights but about an entire society. The Protestant churches were laying claim in it to judge and regulate, at least implicitly, the affairs of the state. Such claims were all the more damaging for the National Party in that they questioned the myth grounded in the NGK that the state was indeed governed by Christian principles.

The SACC resolution was immediately seen as a serious threat by those in control of the state apparatus. Even Vorster, the then Prime Minister, saw fit to declare, 'I want seriously to warn those who are playing with fire in this way to rethink before they burn their fingers irrevocably.'[11] At the same time the Minister of Defence, P.W. Botha, said that his department was taking legal opinion on the resolution.[12]

The response of the white parliamentary opposition was not much different. The leader of the United Party and official Opposition, Sir De Villiers Graaff, said that his party believed it was the duty of every South African to assist in the defence of South Africa against aggression, including terrorism.[13] The United Party

11. *Die Burger*, Cape Town, 6 August 1974.
12. *Comment and Opinion*, 9 August 1974.
13. *EcuNews*, 5 August 1974.

spokesperson on defence matters, Mr W. Vause Raw, claimed that encouraging refusal of military service went beyond legitimate political criticism. He condemned churchmen who sought to give terrorism a 'cloaking of sacrilegious respectability'.[14] The attitude of the then small Progressive Party towards the SACC resolution was stated by its spokesperson, Professor F. van Zyl Slabbert, as follows: 'The Progressive Party strongly disagrees with this resolution also because it spreads a defeatist spirit towards peaceful change and because it draws attention away from crucial political issues that are negotiable in our society.'[15]

The media also responded with vigour, led by the government-controlled South African Broadcasting Corporation (SABC), which described the SACC resolution as a menace to the country's security. The Afrikaans press expressed itself in similar fashion. The Pretoria newspaper, *Die Hoofstad*, in a remarkable *ex cathedra* statement, proclaimed, 'Obedience to the authorities is a biblical injunction. Therefore refusal to do military service is not reconcilable with the bible.'[16] But in the main the Afrikaans press declined the role of theologian and was content to express its condemnation in terms, which, though more concrete, were no less emotional. For instance, *Die Oggendblad* indignantly declared: 'This is evidence of disloyalty to South Africa. Even worse, refusal to do military training is a criminal offence. Does it become church leaders to encourage the youth to do this?'[17]

Virtually the entire English press pursued a similar line.[18] Only the *Rand Daily Mail* made an effort to understand the issues dealt with in the SACC resolution. It remarked sympathetically, '. . . It is correct that we should not ask anyone to die for a country unless he is granted the right to live for it too — in the fullest sense of the word.'[19]

While it is impossible to gauge the reaction of conscientious objectors to the SACC resolution, one of the most significant responses (in that it came from people directly affected by the resolution) was a joint statement issued by members of the executive of the National Union of South African Students (NUSAS), a body representing white English-speaking university students. The key part of the statement read as follows:

> It is the young people of South Africa who are being called upon to fight this war. Many of us are questioning two fundamental issues relating to

14. *The Times*, London, 5 August 1974.
15. ibid.
16. *Die Hoofstad*, Pretoria, 1 August 1974.
17. *Die Oggenblad*, 2 August 1974.
18. *The Star*, 3 August 1974.
19. Quoted in *EcuNews*, 5 August 1974.

this conflict. Firstly, the readiness with which the government is committing the people of South Africa to a prolonged war in defence of a system which promotes and protects the interests of whites and which discriminates at all levels against blacks.

Secondly, the repression of organised and peaceful black opposition to the conditions of domination and exploitation in our society has been responsible for black fellow South Africans taking up arms. It could be argued that we are being called upon to fight a civil war, the cause of which is rooted in the inequalities of our society.

If we are to seek sincerely a peaceful resolution to this conflict it is issues such as these which must be openly and fully debated. But the government, through its propaganda, is developing a widespread war psychosis which blindly clings to militarism as the cause of action open for resolving this conflict.

Many of us believe that this war can be avoided if the inequalities in our society are rooted out — if the aspirations of blacks to share equally in the political process and the wealth of the land are met.[20]

Response within the Christian community

Within the churches a split occurred between those who supported the SACC resolution and those who did not. The hierarchies of a number of denominations even went so far as to condemn the resolution.

It was not surprising that the Afrikaner church groups should come out in favour of the government and attack the SACC's stand. And this they did. The brother of the Prime Minister and Moderator of the NGK's General Synod, Dr J.D. 'Koort' Vorster, announced that the NGK rejected the SACC resolution entirely as it did not have scriptural foundation and added 'The language they (the SACC) speak is the language of the World Council of Churches, which is always against war unless it is a leftist war. I do not say these people are communists, but they are playing into the hands of the leftists.'[21] The NGK saw the SACC resolution as encouraging young people to nurture conscientious objection in conflict with Romans 13. In addition, the synod 'recognised the right and privilege of every citizen to defend his people and fatherland and to protect the life and freedom of its citizens'.[22]

The Baptist Union of South Africa followed suit and passed a resolution dissociating itself from the SACC resolution. It disagreed

---

20. *South African Outlook*, Cape Town, August 1974, p.135. This statement was signed by the members of the NUSAS Executive, the Presidents of the Students Representative Councils of the Universities of the Witwatersrand, Cape Town and Natal (Durban and Pietermaritzburg), and the NUSAS Local Chair at Rhodes University.
21. *The Times*, 5 August 1974; *EcuNews*, 5 August 1974.
22. *EcuNews*, 30 October 1974.

with the way that 'conscientious objection was advocated as a means of registering disapproval of the political and social status quo in South Africa'.[23] Similarly, the Executive Commission of the Presbyterian Church of Southern Africa (PCSA) dissociated itself from the SACC resolution, and at least two Presbyterian congregations followed this lead.[24]

But such sentiments were confined to these denominations and one or two smaller ones. Together these groups constituted a minority in the Christian community, were controlled by whites and some were composed entirely or mainly of whites. Moreover, where the membership was not solely white, division within the denomination was apparent. Evidence of this came when the predominantly black Tsonga Presbyterian church passed a resolution supporting the SACC stand.[25] At the same time the large multiracial denominations came out in support of the SACC resolution. In September 1974 the Diocesan Council of the Anglican Diocese in Johannesburg adopted a resolution supporting the SACC stand.[26] Thereafter the Provincial Standing Committee of the CPSA endorsed the SACC resolution.[27] In October 1974 the 115,000-strong Evangelical Lutheran Church (ELC) in Namibia voiced full support for the resolution,[28] and support also came from the ELC's Transvaal Region.[29]

Several prominent leaders in the church also announced their support for the SACC's stand. Amongst these was the Anglican Archbishop Bill Burnet, who remarked:

> I am not dismayed by the SACC resolution on conscientious objection because it faces us with things as they are. It makes us aware of a crisis which is also an opportunity to see things in a new light and respond to the situation in faith and love. We need to grasp the significance of the fact that some black South Africans, many of whom are Christians, are outside our country seeking to change our power structure by force.[30]

In Durban Archbishop Hurley pursued the critical line of just war theory that had so threatened the government, and declared:

> My conclusion is that the people of South Africa should avoid at all costs getting involved in a border war, and that there should be

23. *EcuNews*, 4 September 1974.
24. *EcuNews*, 5 August 1974.
25. *EcuNews*, 27 November 1974.
26. *EcuNews*,11 September 1974.
27. *EcuNews*, 13 November 1974.
28. *EcuNews*, 20 November 1974.
29. *Pro Veritate*, Johannesburg, Christian Institute, December 1974.
30. *EcuNews*, 21 August 1974.

conscientious objection to getting involved in such a war. Yet I know there are people who cannot or will not agree to do this.

In the South African situation, conscientious objection should be adopted as a principle by the churches. I believe that the churches should adopt this view, even at the risk of open confrontation with the government. Confrontation has to occur sometime.

The Archbishop said that his view could be summed up in four brief statements and a conclusion:

1. If South Africa gets involved in a border war, this war will have been provoked by the policy of apartheid.

2. To defend white South African society by force of arms is to defend the policy of apartheid.

3. To defend apartheid is to defend an unjust cause.

4. It is not permissible for Christians to fight an unjust war.

He concluded that: 'Unless we can claim that a strenuous effort has been made to reach understanding between blacks and whites, including liberation movements, conscientious objection seems the only possible Christian stand.'[31]

However, there was one group within the large multiracial denominations which was vehemently opposed to the SACC stand. This was the group of Christian chaplains in the SADF, and included the military chaplains from the English-language denominations, who issued the following joint statement:

> We, the chaplains of the English-language churches serving in the SADF, are dismayed by the decision of the SACC, taken at Hammanskraal, which appeared to encourage South Africans to refuse to serve in the defence of the country. We recognise injustice at levels of our society but believe that the statement that this society is so different from others that it warrants being described as basically unjust and violent, is unfounded and ill-considered. We therefore dissociate ourselves from this resolution. The SADF has never demanded anything else from us but the proclamation of the Word of God and the pastoral care of the members of our various denominations in the SADF. We, as chaplains in the SADF, who are familiar with the aims, objects and methods of the communistically inspired terrorists who by murder and force attempt to gain access to our land, urge every member of our churches and especially the young men to make their personal contribution in the defence of the country.[32]

Nevertheless it was quite clear that, despite the significant opposition, the majority within the churches supported the SACC resolution. As

---

31. Quoted in *Church and Conscience*, pp.15-16.
32. Quoted by P.W. Botha in the House of Assembly, *Hansard*, 15 August 1974, col. 803-804.

the then Secretary General of the SACC, Mr John Rees, said in response to all the heated reactions, 'It should be remembered that of the ten million Christians in fellowship with the SACC, 85% are black and to date practically every black who has reacted has stood solidly behind this resolution.[33]

Silencing the churches

Even before the SACC conference a Defence Further Amendment Bill had been drafted to modify various aspects of the 1957 Defence Act. When the SACC adopted its controversial resolution the Minister of Defence withdrew the draft bill and added a clause which was calculated to eliminate what the government felt was a threat, as manifested in the SACC resolution. The new clause was enacted and became section 121(c) of the 1957 Act.[34] It provided that a person commits an offence if he 'uses any language or does any act or thing with intent to recommend to, encourage, aid, incite, instigate, suggest to or otherwise cause any other person or any category of persons or persons in general to refuse or fail to render any service to which such other person or a person of such category or persons in general is or are liable or may become liable in terms of this Act'. The maximum sentence for a contravention of this section is a fine of up to R5,000 or imprisonment of up to six years, or both.

Speaking about the clause during the second reading of the bill in the all-white parliament, Defence Minister Botha said that its provisions were aimed at 'those persons who, wrapped in a cloak of sanctimoniousness, are trying to prejudice the security of South Africa'.[35] However, the bill had the inconvenient effect of blurring the distinction between outright pacifism and a position based on the injustice of the South African state. This meant that the churches could be deceptively united in reaction to it. A panic reaction, it was to cost the state dear in the polarisation of church opposition, and precipitated a major church-state clash. The Administrative Board of the Southern African Catholic Bishops' Conference (SACBC) declared in September 1974 that should the Defence Further Amendment Bill become law in its present form, it would be bound in conscience to disobey it, and would likewise expect clergy and people of their own and other churches to do the same.[36] At the same meeting where they expressed their support for the SACC resolution, the 81

---

33. EcuNews, 5 August 1974.
34. Inserted by section 10 of the Defence Further Amendment Act, No.83 of 1974.
35. Survey of Race Relations 1974, Johannesburg, South African Institute of Race Relations (SAIRR), 1975, p.59.
36. EcuNews, 4 September 1974.

pastors of the Transvaal Region of the ELC (which has an almost entirely black membership of 200,000) passed a resolution expressing a broad pacifist argument: 'The Assembly affirms that if the Defence Further Amendment Bill ever becomes law in South Africa, it will invite defiance from those who believe that war and violence are not in accordance with the teaching of Christ . . . The Assembly rejects all legislation which compels a person to do what he believes to be morally wrong because the state sees it as politically right'.[37] Church leaders around the country stood up and spoke out against the new legislation. The proposer of the SACC resolution, Rev. Douglas Bax, described it as an 'extreme' totalitarian attack on the right of freedom of speech.[38]

The editor of the Methodist journal *Dimension*, Rev. Peter Storey, remarked, 'The Bill calls not for patriotism but a blind subservience which, in my view, can be more dangerous to the health of our nation than dissent'.[39] The leaders of the Christian Institute (CI) also featured prominently in church opposition to the Act. The Director of the CI and seconder of the SACC resolution, Dr Beyers Naude, correctly forecast that

> The drastic penalties proposed in the new Defence Further Amendment Bill, if passed, will certainly act as a deterrent to individuals who have basic objections to military service to express their true feelings on the matter of conscientious objection. But it does in no way resolve the crisis of conscience facing many young people who are utterly opposed to the unjust society which is ours, and who are called upon to defend this system by force of arms.[40]

At the same time Rev. Brian Brown, Administrative Director of the CI, made it clear that the church would not be intimidated into silence: 'The state, through its creation of an apartheid society the defence of which is questionable for many Christians, has created a growing crisis of conscience. Having brought about this moral conflict, the state now seeks to legislate as to what guidance the church may give its followers. But the church dares not be silenced on matters as profound as the taking of another's life'.[41] Other leaders shared these sentiments, amongst them the CI's Cape Director, Dr Theo Kotze, who said,

37. *EcuNews*, 2 October 1974.
38. *Rand Daily Mail*, Johannesburg, 15 August 1974.
39. ibid.
40. *Rand Daily Mail*, 15 August 1974.
41. ibid.

The implications of the Bill are terribly serious for the whole church . . . The Bill restricts our pastoral duty, it inhibits the counselling of ministers and others. We cannot under any circumstances surrender our duty to be pastors to the flock of Christ and we must make this known. We dare not surrender the right to encourage young people to face moral issues and there are serious moral issues at stake. The enormous penalties the Bill prescribes do not cancel the imperative of obedience to our Lord.[42]

Despite all the protests the Bill became law, but just before it did, P.W. Botha gave some indication of his approach on the issue when he explained to parliament that: 'I am not going to detail policemen to keep an eye on these people . . . We shall soon find out whether the opinions being exchanged between priests or clergymen and young people and between parents and their children are honest, or whether it is in fact something else that has crept in under the guise of priestly garb. For that reason I am not going to appoint people to keep an eye on parents to see that they do not speak to their children'.[43] There was one consolation when the Bill became law. The Bill had initially provided for a maximum penalty of a R10,000 fine or ten years' imprisonment or both for any contravention of section 121(c). In response to the heated reactions these penalties were reduced to their current form, but still remained severe.

So far the huge penalties prescribed for a contravention of this section have rendered enforcement almost totally unnecessary. Most groups and individuals involved in the war resistance issue in South Africa have become ultra-cautious about public statements on the issue since the section came into effect. This is evidenced by their diligent search for legal advice whenever the question is discussed. Despite the brave words, no church leader has gone to jail under the Act, though some have been banned. At the very least then, section 121(c) has emerged as a serious inhibiting factor in the debate on conscientious objection.

Military Service and War Resistance since 1974

1974 was a watershed in relations between church and state on military matters. It was also a turning point in a number of other respects. In April the Lisbon coup had marked the beginning of a radical political realignment in southern Africa. By the end of the year it was clear that

---

42. *The Times of Zambia*, Lusaka, 19 September 1974.
43. *Hansard*, 29 October 1974, col. 6880-81.

the period of Portuguese colonialism in Africa was coming to an end, and that the buffer of white states which shielded apartheid society from independent Africa, had been irreparably breached. It was now apparent that white rule, which had formerly been considered — at least by the whites — to be invincible, could be overthrown.

In June 1975 Mozambique became independent, while in Angola the MPLA was opposed by the forces of UNITA and FNLA in a bloody conflict. White South Africa, encouraged by leading Western countries such as France and the United States, allied itself with the CIA, and the Zaire dictator Mobutu, in a massive effort to put the small pro-Western armies of FNLA and UNITA in control of the country by Independence Day, 11 November. Initial support to these groups by South Africa, in the form of arms and training, rapidly escalated into a major invasion of Angola by the SADF from its bases in illegally occupied Namibia.

After several months of heavy fighting, Angolan forces of the MPLA government, backed by Cuban arms and troops, stopped the South African invaders 200 km south of Luanda and began to drive them southwards. Overwhelmed by superior forces, unwilling to commit their entire military potential and deserted by their Western allies, the South Africans were forced to retreat. No matter how the apartheid government tried to explain the withdrawal, white South Africa could only experience it as a tremendous defeat, particularly as it provided a considerable psychological boost to all those, within and without the country, who are committed to the overthrow of white domination in southern Africa.

Within months of the South African withdrawal from Angola the apartheid regime was racked by the first waves of the urban uprisings which began on 16 June 1976. Over the next six months the government brutally fought to maintain control and both the para-military police and the army were mobilised. With the same systematic brutality which it had displayed at the time of Sharpeville 16 years before, the regime ruthlessly suppressed all resistance and a semblance of order was restored.

The results of the severe shock of the 1974-1976 events were the 'total strategy' policies of 1977. Pretoria's attempts to find allies in independent Africa had failed miserably; the white buffer had partially collapsed and the armed struggle in Zimbabwe had intensified considerably. White South Africa began to batten down the hatches and dig itself in for a conflict which it now regarded as inevitable. With the militarisation of the apartheid state came a tightening and extension of the military apparatus and its hold on society, and a corresponding increase in the incidence of war resistance.

War resistance after 1974

Since 1974 South African war resisters have opted for two main courses of action in their resistance to military service. Probably about 50% have fled the country and gone into exile, while the rest have remained in the country, most being imprisoned or rendering military service in a non-combatant capacity, and many being constantly on the run from the authorities. The exiles are mainly persons who have resisted conscription as part of a political opposition to apartheid, and those in prison are mainly Christian pacifists or members of recognised religious pacifist sects.

(a) Resisters in exile

It is impossible to calculate the precise number of war resisters in exile, but some idea of order of magnitude can be obtained from the following statistics.

In 1978 the Minister of Defence informed parliament that in 1975, 1976 and 1977 the number of persons who failed to render service in the SADF was 3,314, 3,566, and 3,814 respectively.[44] The corresponding figure for 1978 was 3,123.[45] Of these numbers 605, 916 and 532 were convicted in 1975, 1976 and 1977 respectively.[46] Of the total of 3,123 in 1978, 1,250 gave acceptable reasons for their failure, 284 were prosecuted and the other 1,589 cases were still under investigation when these figures were revealed.[47] So there are a large number of persons who are not officially accounted for. In 1975 the number of such persons was 2,719. The corresponding figures for 1976, 1977 and 1978 are 2,668, 3,307 and 1,589 respectively. These figures represent the *maximum* number of war resisters who could have fled the country. But on the basis of the 1978 breakdown it would be fair to presume that the maximum number of young people unaccounted for does not exceed half of those who have failed to serve. This gives a more realistic maximum for the period 1975-78 of about 5,900. However, the total number of war resisters in exile is likely to be lower than this as many conscripts are known to be evading the authorities inside South Africa.[48] The numbers failing to turn up since 1978 are likely to have increased. In 1980 a defector from South African intelligence disclosed that the department of military intelligence was expecting 5,000 conscripts to fail to render service that year.

---

44. *Hansard*, 17 February 1978, Questions and Replies, col. 181-2.
45. *Hansard*, 22 February 1979, Questions and Replies, col. 157-8.
46. *Annual Survey of Race Relations 1977*, 1978.
47. *Hansard*, 17 February 1978, Questions and Replies, col. 181-2.
48. *Conscientious Objection in South Africa*, Durban, Ad Hoc Committee, 1980, p.13.

War resisters have fled to a variety of countries, including Lesotho, Swaziland, Botswana, Zimbabwe, Mozambique, the USA, Canada, Israel, Australia, New Zealand, West Germany, Norway, the Netherlands and Britain. In the main their principal reasons for refusing to serve are based on political objections to fighting for apartheid, in some cases heightened by the probability of combat in Namibia or border areas. While many of them are Christians, they do not usually express their decision to leave in formal Christian terms. Many war resisters are able to remain in their country of exile as immigrants, students, or by virtue of their ancestry. A few hundred of them have sought political asylum, mainly in Britain and the Netherlands, where they have organised themselves into self-help organisations, and, linking up with anti-apartheid groups, have campaigned in support of war resisters in South Africa. In Britain and the Netherlands the war resisters' organisation is known as the Committee on South African War Resistance (COSAWR).

(b) Resisters inside the country

In addition to the unknown number who are on the run, a small number of war resisters who have remained in South Africa are conscientious non-combatants. Although they do render service in the SADF, they refuse to do so in a combatant capacity. Many are Christians with most belonging to the small recognised pacifist denominations such as the Seventh Day Adventists and Plymouth Brethren. In recent years more members of the major denominations have opted for non-combatant service.

By far the largest known number of war resisters who have remained in South Africa consists of those who are charged with refusing to render military service. In 1973 159 persons, all but one of them Jehovah's Witnesses were convicted and imprisoned.[49] The corresponding figure for the first six months of 1974 was 122, comprising 120 Jehovah's Witnesses and two Christadelphians.[50] For the period after 1974 the figures released by the Minister of Defence give rise to some confusion. This is no doubt due to the National Party definition of conscientious objection, which confines the meaning of the term to only those objectors who are members of recognised religious denominations 'by the tenets whereof their members may not participate in war'. For instance, in 1975, of a total of 605 persons (a drastic rise over the figures for preceding years owing to the invasion of Angola) convicted for refusing to render military service, P.W.

---

49. P.W. Botha in the House of Assembly, *Hansard*, 13 September 1974, Questions and Replies, col. 448-450.
50. ibid. No figures are available for the last six months of 1974.

Botha stated that only 150 advanced 'conscientious objection' to service as a ground for their refusal, while none 'indicated that default was due to adherence to a religious denomination'.[51]

In 1976 and 1977 respectively 916 and 532 persons were convicted for refusing to render military service and of these totals Mr P.W. Botha announced that only 95 and 86 persons respectively 'advanced conscientious objection to service as a ground for such failure'. He added that in 1976 none 'indicated that their default was due to adherence to a religious denomination', while in 1977 only one person, a member of the NGK, did.[52] Yet according to Mr Botha in 1978, after a mere half of the cases had been processed, of 284 persons who were prosecuted 110 advanced conscientious objection as ground for their failure to render service, and of these, 55 were Jehovah's Witnesses. According to the Minister the remaining 55 had 'other conscientious objections'.[53]

In 1981 General Malan announced that 110 people had given religious grounds for their refusal to perform military service, mostly Jehovah's Witnesses.[54] However, in 1980 Mr Botha revealed to parliament that as of 22 April of that year, the Detention Barracks held 420 inmates of whom five had been convicted for desertion and 130 for 'neglect of duty', and 243 for being absent without leave (awol).[55] Presumably 'neglect of duty' refers to war resistance as it contrasts with the category 'dereliction of duty' mentioned in the same set of statistics. In February 1982 it was disclosed that of the 577 people in military Detention Barracks at the time, 312 were detained for refusing to undergo military training and 207 for being 'absent without leave'.[56] It may thus be deduced that in any given year a large proportion of those in Detention Barracks will be detained either for desertion or for war resistance. While many will be Jehovah's Witnesses, a large number will be individuals unwilling to make an issue of their reasons for refusing to serve. Of these it would be fair to assume that a significant percentage had either political or religious objections.

51. *Hansard*, 17 February 1978, Questions and Replies, col. 181-2.
52. ibid.
53. *Hansard*, 22 February 1979, Questions and Replies, col. 157-8.
54. *The Citizen*, 6 February 1982; the Department of Defence recognises the following denominations as 'peace churches': Jehovah's Witnesses, Plymouth Brethren, Christadelphians, Suppliant Faithists and Seventh Day Adventists (*Survey of Race Relations 1980*, p.208).
55. *Survey of Race Relations 1980*, p.208.
56. *The Star*, 27 February 1982.

3. The Politics of Conscientious Objection

In South Africa war resistance is not regarded by the authorities as an apolitical, moral or religious phenomenon, as some Western governments regard it. True, spokesmen of the apartheid regime appear to make a rather simplistic distinction between conscientious objectors who are members of recognised pacifist religious denominations, and on the other hand, all other types of conscientious objectors. The latter are accused of being unwilling to render any type of national service whatsoever and are therefore seen as a threat, while the former are accorded some form of recognition and relief within the military system (even if only informally).[1] (This is, of course, unjust as many objectors would be willing to perform some kind of community service, outside the military system.) The explanation for this distinction is not difficult to find. The government insists that national service be performed in a military context because it regards conscientious objection not accommodated within the military system as a threat to South Africa's 'defence capabilities'. Concern about this has been expressed by government spokesmen on a number of occasions.[2] In March 1978 deputy Minister of Defence Coetsee declared:

> What we cannot tolerate or allow, however, is for a person who has a religious objection to use that objection as a pretext to evade national service and on that basis fail to report when he is called up to do national service. I am saying this particularly because an objection of this kind — as was proved in the war in Vietnam — can be used as an excuse for completely undermining national service and frustrating the defence of the country in the long run as a consequence.[3]

---

1. On this distinction see the statements made in parliament by P.W. Botha (*Hansard*, 26 August 1974, col. 1476 and 1484; and 28 March 1978, col. 3318) and Deputy Minister of Defence, H.J. Coetsee (*Hansard*, 28 March 1978, col. 3295).
2. See *Hansard*, 24 May 1972, col. 7971; 26 August 1974, col. 1485; and 29 October 1974, col. 6853.
3. *Hansard*, 28 March 1978, col. 3295.

Thus conscientious objectors are accorded recognition only as long as they can be accommodated within the SADF. Any type of war resistance which cannot be harnessed to promote the war effort is unacceptable to the government and, worse, is branded as subversive.

Although the military authorities have accorded non-combatant status to some objectors who are not members of the recognised 'peace churches', it is not SADF policy to do so, as it is in the case of 'peace church' members. The reasons for this policy are as follows:

a. The policy of according non-combatant status to members of recognised religious pacifist sects ensures that recognition is only officially accorded to objectors whose opposition to participation in the war effort stems from an absolute objection to participation in war in general, and thus cannot be readily interpreted as a particular objection to service in the SADF. A policy of granting such status to other objectors would be open to the latter interpretation.

b. The government fears that an extension of this policy to cover other objectors would lead to an increase in the number of applications for non-combatant status.[4]

Although the government may not be aware of the finer points of conscientious objection, it fully realises the political implications of this form of civil disobedience. Nowhere is this more clearly illustrated than in the 1974 debate on section 121(c) of the Defence Act. In this debate Mr P.W. Botha quoted with approval a comment made by the former Prime Minister and Minister of Defence of France, Michel Debré. Debré had said, 'Pacifism is a very old form of political protest. How can one not be sympathetic towards it? Let us, however, look at reality. First of all pacifism can become a means for obtaining certain goals besides peace. Many *democratic* leaders and agitators are not pacifists, but abuse words, ideas and emotive choices of pacifism to rise in the world and, if the opportunity arises, to gain power'.[5] Pacifism is in itself seen as a threat to apartheid's defence capabilities. This is quite evident from Mr P.W. Botha's comment on Debré's statement: 'Here, I think, Mr Debré laid his finger on the root of the evil experienced by the Western world today, for these doctrines are not tolerated behind the Iron Curtain. Behind the Iron Curtain nobody will be allowed to undermine the defence force of China, Russia or Czechoslovakia, but in the Western world there are enough lackeys of the communistic doctrines who are engaged in this kind of undermining while wrapping themselves in a cloak of sanctimoniousness'.[6]

---

4. See *Hansard*, 29 October 1974, col. 6855.
5. *Hansard*, 15 August 1974, col. 801.
6. ibid.

Thus even the pacifist form of conscientious objection is credited with attributed political consequences and motives, whether intended or not by pacifist objectors. And, indeed, in the context of the total demands of National Security State doctrine, the pacifist's opting out does have political significance. Any objection to service in the SADF, for whatever reasons, is essentially opposed to the role of the military in South Africa. Such a situation arises from the inseparable link between the SADF and the system which it is required to maintain. In this sense the South African authorities' position has been quite consistent.

Clamp-down on War Resistance

Faced with the radical alteration of political alignments in Southern Africa after 1974, Pretoria felt compelled to enlarge its pool of military manpower. In addition to plans to double the size of the Permanent Force, in 1978, the Defence Act was amended to replace section 126a with stricter provisions to deal with the growing resistance to military service.[7]

The new provisions entrenched the privileged status of 'peace church' members in two ways:

a. Where such persons are concerned the Act now distinguishes between failure to perform the initial period of military service and failure to attend the subsequent camps. Where the failure to render service involves a period of less than 12 months, such an objector need only serve 18 months' imprisonment as opposed to a 36-month sentence for failure to render military service of, or in excess of, 12 months.

b. The Act also now provides that an unlawful conscientious objector belonging to a recognised religious pacifist sect may not again be charged for failing to render military service, if he is serving or has served detention for such failure.

All other war resisters are liable on conviction to a fine not exceeding R2,000 or to imprisonment for a period not exceeding two years or to both fine and imprisonment. The same penalty is provided irrespective of whether the failure to render military service involves the initial two-year period of service or a camp. Moreover, war resisters in general may again be called up for service after completing their sentence, and may be charged again and again for each failure to render military service when called up to do so, until such time as they are no longer liable to render military service, that is, until their 66th birthday.

7. Defence Amendment Act, No.49 of 1978.

The application and enforcement of the law has also been tightened up and taken over by the military. Prior to the 1978 legislation it was standard practice for the military to handle 'peace church' members as military offenders, while all other objectors were dealt with under civilian process. Members of the 'peace churches' were tried by a military court and served their sentence in Detention Barracks. This was a standard practice which developed through agreements between the hierarchies of these denominations and the military authorities. Other resisters were tried in civilian courts which were not subject to the Military Discipline Code (MDC) except insofar as the nature of the sentence was concerned. But in 1978 the position of this latter group of objectors changed. They are now treated as military offenders and are subject to the very military structures which they oppose.

The area where the military's clamp-down became most noticeable was in the Detention Barracks. Here, where Jehovah's Witnesses and members of other religious pacifist groups once fought the SADF for recognition, a new arena of conflict between church and state opened, as members of the larger denominations began their battle for recognition.

Escalation of the Conflict

When the church took up the issue of war resistance in 1974 it encountered a reaction from the state which was so hostile that a major confrontation between church and state threatened to develop. The church was not prepared for such a situation, as was revealed by the major split between denominations and between hierarchies and the grass roots, which the SACC resolution and government response occasioned. Nevertheless, it was clear that if the church was to focus on conscientious objection in the future, conflict between it and the state would be inevitable.

The church and war resistance after 1974

The first comprehensive statement by a single denomination on conscientious objection emerged from the Methodist Church of Southern Africa (MCSA) at its annual conference held shortly after the SACC conference in 1974. This statement read as follows:

> This Conference
> a. Resolves that Christian opinion has always been divided on the question of how Christians ought to respond to the call to bear arms in times of war or national crisis, and that this division still exists.

44

b. Affirms that the position of the conscientious objector has a legitimate place within the Christian tradition and that the right to discuss, question or advocate this position must be regarded as an integral part of the religious liberty fundamental to the health of our society.

c. Acknowledges that the South African government has made provision for certain categories of conscientious objectors either through

(i) the option of 'non-combatant' duties, or

(ii) in the case of refusal to wear military uniform at all, a single prison sentence.

d. Seeks a reconsideration of the latter provision (ii), suggesting that there are creative and useful ways whereby such conscientious objectors might serve their country.

e. Points out that conscientious objection is not always based on purely pacifist convictions, but has sometimes arisen through the peculiar circumstances of a specific conflict, leading a person to refuse service because of his inability to share or accept the relative 'rightness' of the cause for which he is called to fight, and that the present conflict on our borders provides no exception.[8]

This statement was the only considered attempt by a denomination to follow the SACC lead and to provide guidance on the issue to its members. Most of the other hierarchies were occupied in formulating responses to either the SACC resolution or the new legislation, and therefore failed to clarify their positions to their membership, let alone challenge their members to be conscientious objectors. In this respect the Methodist statement appeared as a lone if timid voice in the wilderness. Although cautious in its approach and modest in its demands, this statement foreshadowed the future leading role of the Methodist hierarchy in relation to other denominational hierarchies, a development which has its foundation in the democratic structures of the Methodist Church and the emergence within it of a powerful black caucus.

After the furore raised by the SACC resolution had subsided somewhat and the section 121(c) of the Defence Act had become law, the church, stunned by the state's untempered ferocity, relegated the war resistance issue to backroom committees. Attempts to commit the church to a constructive programme of action met with failure. Not even the SACC remained unafflicted by caution. At its National Conference at Hammanskraal in 1975, Rev. Douglas Bax again proposed a motion dealing with conscientious objection and a strategy for the church in the future. John Rees, then SACC General Secretary, expressed (in absentia) strong opposition to the motion and

---

8. Quoted in *Church and Conscience*, p.10.

it was agreed to refer the motion to the Executive for consideration. Mr Bax argued against this referral, describing it as a 'cop-out'. The Anglican Bishop of Natal, Philip Russell, then proposed, and the conference resolved, that the motion be treated as confidential and be dealt with by various divisions of the Council for consideration.[9]

At the half-yearly meeting of the SACC's Justice and Reconciliation Committee in September 1975, Rev. Joe Wing, secretary of the United Congregational Church of Southern Africa (UCCSA), read a paper on conscientious objection. He argued that conscientious objection should be taken further than military service and should be seen broadly as a form of protest against the violation of human rights. He declared that: 'Conscientious objection as a positive power of passive resistance has not yet been practised on a wide enough scale for its full impact to be felt'.[10] This contention was duly discussed but church hierarchies paid scant attention to the sentiments. At the 1976 National Conference of the SACC the war resistance issue received only passing mention when it was suggested that the Council 'look in depth at methods of non-violent opposition'.[11]

In February 1976 the Southern African Catholic Bishops Conference (SACBC) requested its Administrative Board to institute an investigation into the accepted attitude to conscientious objection in the South African armed forces, and to explore the possibility of establishing an ecumenical agency to help safeguard the position of conscientious objectors.[12] Meanwhile war resistance had not entirely ceased to be an issue in other denominations either, although it did become less prominent.

The churches develop their doctrine
The rise of black consciousness and the outbreak of the 1976 popular uprising had a dramatic radicalising effect on the church. Church ministers were unavoidably drawn into the upheaval, church buildings were used as meeting places, and church gatherings (including funerals) were forcibly broken up by the police. The churches came under enormous pressure to take sides and to stand up for justice. Black theologians and ministers were no longer content with pious platitudes from their white hierarchies and a small group of committed white church members were equally impatient with the hierarchies' futile attempts to avoid a confrontation between church

---

9. *EcuNews*, 23 July 1975.
10. *EcuNews*, 25 September 1975.
11. *EcuNews*, 4 August 1976.
12. *EcuNews*, 18 February 1976.

and state. These groups demanded that the hierarchies speak out with clarity to state their position and provide guidance to their denominations.

But the first steps were tentative; in September 1976 the Natal Diocesan Synod of the CPSA passed a resolution calling on the government to investigate and establish 'additional alternatives to military service' in the form of community service which would benefit all South Africans. The resolution went on to encourage all people to make a moral choice on the use of violence for maintaining or changing the status quo. It recognised the right of each individual to follow the dictates of his or her Christian conscience as well as the church's responsibility for these people.[13]

Then, in February 1977, after some discussion in Catholic youth and student groups, the SACBC issued an important statement on war resistance and became the second major denomination in South Africa to declare publicly its support for the right of every individual to object to military service on grounds of conscience. While it did not specifically link the decision to become a war resister to the issue of justice, other statements made by the Catholic bishops in 1977 left no doubt about the Conference's assessment of apartheid society. The key parts of the text of this statement are as follows:

> In the armed struggle that is developing on our borders and which could easily spread internally a grievous situation arises for all who are concerned about the use of violence. On the one side the conviction grows in a significant sector of the oppressed majority that only violence will bring liberation. On the other, the minority in power sees itself threatened by indiscriminate violence supported by international Communism.
>
> In these agonising circumstances we can only promise with God's help to give leadership in an ongoing Christian examination of this tragic situation. We intend to publish reflections from time to time as incentives to Christian prayer, thought and commitment and we hope to be able to do this with the representatives of other Christian churches and organisations. In the meantime we have resolved to say something about conscientious objection.
>
> According to the teaching of the Second Vatican Council, 'it seems just that laws should make humane provision for the case of conscientious objectors who refuse to carry arms, provided they accept some other form of community service' (Constitution 'The Church in the Modern World', No.79).
>
> In order to understand the issue of conscientious objection, a careful distinction should be made between universal conscientious objection (the pacifist) and selective conscientious objection (e.g. on the

---

13. *EcuNews*, 10 September 1976.

grounds that a particular war is unjust); between combatant military service (carrying arms) and non-combatant military service (e.g. in the medical corps) and between military service (combatant or non-combatant) and national service (which could include services to the community, like social welfare, education, housing).

In this matter of conscientious objection we defend the right of every individual to follow his own conscience, the right therefore to conscientious objection both on the grounds of universal pacifism and on the grounds that he seriously believes the war to be unjust. In this, as in every other matter, the individual is obliged to make a moral judgment in terms of the facts at his disposal after trying to ascertain these facts to the best of his ability. While we recognise that the conscientious objector will have to suffer the consequences of his own decision and the penalties imposed by the state, we uphold his right to do this and we urge the state to make provision for alternative forms of non-military national service as is done in other countries in the world.[14]

The Catholic statement with its emphasis on individual right met with enthusiastic response from other churches, for it came at a time when the various hierarchies were under increasing pressure to speak out on the issue. Its contents were subsequently endorsed by the CPSA in April 1977,[15] the Methodist Conference in October,[16] and the UCCSA in the same month. The UCCSA added that 'The voice of conscience must not be silenced by the compulsion of government edict or the clamour of popular demand'.[17]

Also in October the Cape Town Diocesan Synod of the CPSA passed a resolution on war resistance which again made the link between justice and conscientious objection:

1. We endorse the words of our Archbishop[18] in his statement to the press (on 16 February 1977) that 'the society we have created for ourselves is morally indefensible. This is very serious at a time when we are being asked to defend it'.

   We sympathise with those who in conscience believe that it is an act of disobedience to God to be part of the military structures of this country because they are convinced that by doing so they would be defending what is morally indefensible.

2. We uphold the right of such people to be conscientious objectors and we urge the state to make provision for alternative forms of non-military service.

   We accept that we, as a church, have a positive duty to make all people aware of what is involved in being used to defend the morally

14. Southern African Catholic Bishops' Conference Plenary Session, February 1977.
15. *EcuNews*, 22 April 1977.
16. *EcuNews*, 28 October 1977.
17. *EcuNews*, 26 October 1977.
18. Archbishop Bill Burnett.

48

indefensible and to challenge each other in the cost of discipleship, putting first the claims of Christ over all our being and doing.[19]

The third and final part of the resolution requested the publication of the resolution's contents within the denomination and urged discussion thereon.

Military chaplains and conscientious objectors

In March 1978 when the government introduced the new section 126a of the Defence Act, the Minister of Defence announced in parliament that the proposed increased prison sentences for war resisters had the support of the majority of denominations represented in the SADF. He said: 'All the churches of South Africa are represented in the Defence Force. The majority of these churches — that is, of their representatives — have considered and have agreed with this measure'.[20] Spokesmen for two major denominations immediately stressed that support from SADF chaplains for the increased prison sentences did not necessarily mean official church support for these measures. The provincial executive officer of the CPSA, Canon Michael Carmichael, said that if there had been official consultation with the church, he did not know of it.[21] In the Methodist Church, Rev. Austen Massey, secretary of the Christian Citizenship Department, which is responsible for the issue of conscientious objection in the Methodist Church, remarked, 'I don't think the church would in any way approve of increased sentences'.[22]

Interestingly enough it was also revealed in March that the SADF's Permanent Force chaplains from the English-language denominations had recommended that the government make provision for conscientious objectors who are not members of the recognised 'peace churches'. Amongst them were chaplains from the Catholic, Anglican, Methodist, Congregational, Presbyterian and Baptist denominations. They specifically recommended that the SADF permit such objectors to render military service in a non-combatant capacity and that, in addition, the state introduce a form of civilian national service for those objectors who were opposed to rendering military service.[23]

During 1978 there were also a number of noteworthy developments amongst lay people both within and outside the churches. In Cape Town some leaders from a number of small pacifist

19. Quoted in *Church and Conscience*, pp.8-9.
20. *The Star*, 29 March 1979.
21. ibid.
22. ibid.
23. *EcuNews*, 31 March 1978. See also *The Star*, 27 June 1978.

denominations were joined by a few war resisters from other churches in planning an ambulance service. This was intended as a pilot project to demonstrate the viability of a non-military form of national service. Another initiative came from the gathering of students, directly affected by the question of military service, in the NUSAS National Congress towards the end of the year. The Congress resolved to establish a committee, later known as MILCOM, to:

> investigate the influence of service in the SADF on —
> (i) those facing such service
> (ii) those undergoing such service
> (iii) those who have completed such service
> to investigate the influence of Youth Preparedness Programmes and to explore official alternatives to service in the SADF in the fields of education, medical and community services and to press the government for the implementation thereof.

The Congress further resolved to call on the state to 'lift restrictions imposed on the individual's right to debate conscientious objection, and recognise the right of the individual to decide for himself whether or not to engage in military or in community service'.[24]

By the end of 1978 it was evident that the churches would support the rights of conscientious objectors. This much was evident from the one or two statements which had emanated from the churches in the preceding two years. A significant factor in stiffening this stand was the contact with the mainstream of their theological and doctrinal traditions into which the churches had been brought by the process of working out their positions. This took different forms in the different churches, reflecting their different structures. The Roman Catholic bishops appealed to authoritative Catholic teaching as embodied in the statements of the Second Vatican Council, the 1971 Synod of Bishops and recent popes.[25] In the Anglican and Methodist churches the process tended to work in the opposite direction, with the experience of the South African churches influencing the rest of their communions. The Church of England's International Affairs Committee, a group ultimately responsible to the General Synod, produced a report on South Africa which included a section devoted to conscientious objection and called specifically for support for the war resistance movement.[26] The 1982 British Methodist Conference

---

24. NUSAS National Congress, Cape Town, December 1978.
25. See above, p.47, and the Roman Catholic authorities cited in Neil Mitchell's statement (below, Appendix A, p.90). A comparable use of authoritative statements by a national church can be seen in the statements by the United States Catholic Conference, below, Appendix C, pp.103-109.
26. *Facing the Facts*, London 1982, p.20.

declared its support for the South African Methodists in their stand on conscientious objection, and endorsed their view on the principle involved.[27]

The churches might have defined their position at the level of principles, but their response still did not match developments in society, or even among their own members. War resistance was now a small but growing phenomenon, particularly after the introduction of the increased periods of compulsory service, and an increasing number of people were beginning to focus their attention on it. Sooner or later the churches were going to have to respond to this changing situation with concrete programmes of action. It was apparent that in the face of rapid militarisation this response would come sooner rather than later.

The Growing Response in the Churches

During 1979 war resistance became a prominent issue among students at the white English-language universities in South Africa. An increasing number of young men, many of them students, were leaving the country to avoid military service. They included a number of student leaders. MILCOM, the committee set up by NUSAS, established groups on many of the white English-speaking campuses which brought the issue to the forefront. Focus weeks on war resistance were organised, public debates involving church leaders were held, publications and pamphlets were distributed, and a petition was circulated calling on the government to introduce a non-military form of national service for conscientious objectors. A fair number of MILCOM members were Christians and so were a growing number of people who participated in the committee's activities. Not surprisingly there was an overlap in participation in MILCOM activities and those of Christian organisations dealing with war resistance. In this way the issue also began to receive more attention in Christian student circles.

At the same time a number of off-campus Christian groups sprang up around the country with the intention of working on the war resistance issue and campaigning for the introduction of a non-military form of national service. Although these and the student committee were autonomous groups, their combined effect was to create a greater awareness of the implications of military service in South Africa, to persuade the various denominational hierarchies to take action with regard to the question of war resistance and to provide support for conscientious objectors' groups. Together with

---

27. For the text, see below, Appendix C, p.103.

the courageous stand of conscientious objector Peter Moll, they were to a large extent responsible for the church response which came later that year.

On 11 September, a Baptist, Peter Moll, was tried by a military court and found guilty of failing to report for military service. The case had attracted considerable attention both as a result of press coverage and because Moll had circulated a statement of his reasons for refusal to church leaders around the country. Most observers, including the sympathisers who packed the courtroom, expected a stiff sentence as this was his second unlawful refusal to render military service. But the SADF, in a last attempt to persuade Moll to enter the army, let him off with a fine. Nevertheless, the point had been made.

In the last four months of 1979 there was a spate of resolutions on war resistance from the churches. The first came from the Presbyterian Church of Southern Africa (PCSA) which adopted the strongest stand since the SACC resolution of 1974:

1. The Assembly reasserts the right of the church to debate freely, pro and con, whether it is God's will for the citizens of our country to do military service in the South African Defence Force. It therefore calls on the Minister of Defence to repeal section 121 of the Defence Act which inhibits such free debate and relies on threats and force instead of rational argument.
2. The Assembly instructs every Presbytery to appoint one of its members to be a Counsellor in War and Peace issues who will be specially concerned to promote discussion about war and peace in congregations within its bounds and to provide counsel and information about the options and penalties they face to those contemplating conscientious objection, when they request it.
3. The Assembly deplores the practice of sentencing conscientious objectors to a period or recurring periods in prison or detention barracks. It appeals to the Minister of Defence to amend the law so as to provide an alternative form of national service to military service.[28]

At about the same time the Assembly of the Baptist Union of South Africa adopted a resolution which, while reaffirming the state's 'right to call on its citizens to share in the defence of the country', also recognised 'the right of individuals to express their genuine and sincere objection to taking up arms on the ground of conscience or religious convictions'. It earnestly requested the government to amend the law to make provision for 'persons who, regardless of religious denomination, have a sincere objection to carrying arms and to allow

---

28. Quoted in *Church and Conscience*, p.13.

them to fulfil the service required of them in a non-combatant capacity'. Finally the resolution asked that 'the government should recognise that there are those individuals who, on religious grounds, cannot conscientiously serve in any armed forces and that provision should be made for these persons to serve the community in some civilian capacity for at least an equivalent period of time and in circumstances as similar as possible to those under which service in the armed forces is performed'.[29] An almost identical set of resolutions was proposed by the General Assembly of the UCCSA.[30] The Congregationalists also called for a widespread discussion of the military service issue amongst their congregations.[31]

Then in October at its annual conference the MCSA proposed a procedure for ascertaining whether a person can be classified as a conscientious objector, and resolved that representation be made to the Minister of Defence accordingly. The proposal was limited to members of the church and suggested that a commission of enquiry, comprising 'a fair cross-section representative both of the church and the Department of Defence', be established to test the convictions of any person claiming to be a conscientious objector. In terms of the proposal, a conscientious objector who is recognised as such, would be classified as a non-combatant and should be offered the 'option of service outside the structure of the SADF'. The resolution also announced that, 'The church is emphatic that the classification of such trainees as conscientious objectors be in no way liable to penalisation'.[32]

Finally in November 1979 the Provincial Synod of the CPSA accepted the right of individuals to follow their conscience and fight for a liberation movement and adopted a mild resolution including the following:

2. Requests
a. the Minister of Defence of the Republic of South Africa to create a committee (or some other appropriate procedure) that will enable the Department of Defence to discuss specific proposals and problems which are raised —
(i) by the request for non-combatant forms of military service that a conscientious non-combatant can render with a good conscience, and
(ii) by the request for non-military forms of national service that a conscientious non-militarist can render with a good conscience.

29. ibid., p.14.
30. ibid., p.12.
31. ibid.
32. ibid., pp.11-12.

b. the Synod of Bishops of the CPSA to co-operate with any Committee on Military Service which may be established by the Southern African Catholic Bishops' Conference.
3. Commends to the prayers and the pastoral care of the Church
   a. those men of whatsoever denomination who for conscience sake are paying the penalty for non-compliance with the military duties imposed on them by the state, and
   b. the families of the above men.[33]

Together these statements constituted a firm public stand that the churches had a duty to take up the issue of war resistance and would not be intimidated into ignoring this duty. But, more important, the statements provided the basis for intensive discussion and education within the various congregations of the church, although this did not occur entirely through the channels envisaged by the hierarchies. By this stage most denominations had assigned to either special committees or existing structures the tasks of researching the issue and of initiating the education of the membership. These groups now made some effort to do this, but were unfortunately limited by practical considerations such as the restrictions on time and energy which other responsibilities demanded of their clerical and lay members, together with varying degrees of foot-dragging.

The work was therefore largely left to the unofficial church groups which had emerged during the course of the year. These groups were composed mainly of ministers and members of the major denominations, some of whom were declared objectors. Although they operated autonomously, there was a loose degree of co-operation and contact, both between the various groups and between each and the church structures. Amongst other things these various committees encouraged discussion on war resistance in their respective fields of operation, conducted research into the issue, acted as support groups for objectors, called for alternative national service and campaigned for effective action within the church. Together they formed what was, to all intents and purposes, a conscientious objection movement within the Christian community.

War Resisters in Prison

Perhaps the most dramatic expression of the conflict between church and state on the issue of war resistance took place in connection with the resistance to military service of the two Baptist objectors, Peter Moll and Richard Steele. Without the protection of priestly cloth or

---

33. ibid., pp.9-10.

parliamentary privilege, these two men laid bare the reality of state persecution of conscientious objectors. Moll, who had been fined for refusing to attend a camp in September 1979, was called up to another camp the very next month. Again he refused to attend, basing his objections more firmly on a refusal to defend apartheid. He was then arrested by the military police and called to stand trial before a military court. In a letter to his commanding officer in which he explained the reasons for his resistance, Moll summarised the grounds for his objection as follows:

> Selective conscientious objection is the refusal to engage in a particular war, while making no necessary statement about war in general. I have decided to be a selective conscientious objector because:
> a. In terms of Christian moral standards, South African society is fundamentally unjust.
> b. The insurgents are generally not foreigners but South African citizens — i.e. the situation is one of civil war.
> c. This makes one question very seriously just what one is required to fight for, and what one is required to die for.[34]

The trial was given much publicity as it struck at the heart of the national security state and appeared as a test case for the churches' 'just war' position. On 4 December the SADF court sentenced Moll to 18 months' detention in Detention Barracks. Church leaders, including Bishop Desmond Tutu, the General Secretary of the SACC, the Catholic Archbishops of Cape Town, Pretoria and Durban, the Anglican Bishop and Suffragan Bishop of Natal and various Methodist, Congregational and NGK ministers, immediately issued a statement in which they noted with concern the arrest and detention of Peter Moll. They pointed out that 'he was a conscientious objector to military service in the present situation of South Africa because he is convinced that South African society is fundamentally unjust and that military service would involve him in violent conflict with citizens of South Africa who suffer under the prevailing injustices'. They declared that, 'it is well known to us that there are many young men facing the same dilemma as Peter Moll, that is, whether to undertake military service in conflict with their conscience or whether to suffer the harsh penalty of refusal'. The statement continued:

> We plead with the government to understand that in the present circumstances of our country, conscientious objection can be based on genuine religious and moral convictions.
> If the Prime Minister himself is convinced that change is necessary

---

34. *The Cape Times*, Cape Town, 5 December 1979.

before injustice drives people to revolution, surely others have the right to claim that their perception of the injustice around them gives them the right to conscientious objection.

We plead with the government at the earliest possible opportunity to regularise the position of conscientious objectors through the provision of alternative non-military forms of national service and in the meantime to exercise in regard to Peter Moll and all other conscientious objectors the humanity and clemency that should be characteristic of a Christian society.[35]

The public outcry had some effect. The military authorities were apprehensive lest Moll be but the first of a new breed of objectors and they were reluctant to repeat their embarrassing experience with the uncompromising Jehovah's Witnesses of earlier years. Their determination to crush war resistance had now left them with a new potential martyr on their hands. From their experience they knew that such martyrdom was likely to be contagious and the last thing they needed was the emergence of resisters as articulate as Moll, a development which threatened to undermine their militarisation programme. Accordingly, Moll's sentence was reduced to 12 months.

But, as the military later found out, the problem was not to be so easily dispensed with. Within Detention Barracks Moll continued his objection by refusing to wear the regulation military dress and perform military drill. The SADF felt that it had to stop this resistance. Moll was therefore sent to solitary confinement and, when he still maintained his objection, he was subjected to a series of two-week spells in solitary confinement which threatened to continue for the duration of his sentence. News of this and the stark conditions in Detention Barracks began to leak out to the churches.

At the end of February 1980 Richard Steele, a pacifist who also specifically opposed the defence of the unjust system in South Africa, was convicted for failing to render military service and was sentenced to one year in Detention Barracks. Both he and Peter Moll had insisted on their readiness to render an alternative non-military form of national service and both had made several concrete attempts to do this, the most noteworthy being in the ambulance project of the Cape Town pacifist group. But the state rejected these moves. For instance, in November 1979 Steele accompanied two other persons to the 'operational area' in northern Namibia to establish an ambulance service there. The party was met by South African security police, issued with an order banning them from the area, and escorted out.[36] This commitment to render non-military national service obviously

---

35. ibid.
36. *The Star*, 26 November 1979.

strengthened their cases in the public's eyes.

In Detention Barracks Steele joined Moll in refusing to wear military dress and perform military drill. For their pains the two objectors were repeatedly punished for continuing the very resistance which had led to their imprisonment in the first place. The military authorities made it quite clear that these additional punishments would continue until the objectors abandoned their convictions. Thus they were not a little concerned when Moll and Steele were joined in their resistance by two other objectors who were in Detention Barracks.

The plight of Moll and Steele proved to be a rallying point which united sympathisers around the country in a common resolve to campaign for a just disposition for war resisters and to urge the hierarchies of the various denominations to do the same. It was also a live issue which touched many white Christians, mainly youth. At the English-language universities traditionally apolitical evangelical students were suddenly compelled to confront the repression of two of their number. Some were forced for the first time to examine the reasons for the objectors' resistance and to question their own previously unconsidered positions.

Finally in August 1980, after spending a total of 125 days in solitary confinement, Moll received a partial reprieve when an SADF spokesman announced that it had been decided to give him 'the benefit of the doubt' and that henceforth he would be treated as a 'peace church' conscientious objector for the duration of his sentence. This meant that he was no longer required to wear the regulation military dress and perform military drill. Similar privileges were accorded to Steele.[37] The church hailed this as a victory.

The State's Propaganda War

From the time it began its military expansion in the early 1960s, the apartheid regime has waged an incessant propaganda campaign to justify the build-up and to unite whites in defence of their privileged position. With monotonous regularity government ministers have warned of external threats and a communist conspiracy to reduce the country to the status of a Soviet satellite. In the early 1970s Pretoria intensified its propaganda war to complement its renewed efforts to militarise South African society. When resistance to military service grew to the point where the state began to regard it as a threat, it too became a specific subject of government propaganda. Already in 1970

---

37. *The Sunday Times*, Johannesburg, 10 August 1980; *The Sunday Tribune*, Durban, 10 August 1980.

Minister of Defence P.W. Botha, probably angered by the militant resistance of the Jehovah's Witnesses, found it necessary to declare that 'The honour and duty to defend one's country should not be made subservient to one's religious convictions'.[38]

Further controversy was aroused in 1972 by a National Party MP, Dr G. de V. Morrison,[39] who, while commenting in parliament on the new provisions governing war resistance, warned: 'If we . . . want to make provision for "basic human rights" or "freedom of conscience" we are most certainly heading for a situation that borders on anarchy'.[40] Not content with this, Morrison continued a little further on in the same debate: 'Conscience is not, nor was it ever, the highest authority . . . To speak of "basic human rights" or of "freedom of conscience" in times such as these, in which we are being threatened by the aggressive communism of both the Peking and Moscow varieties where our security and survival are virtually being threatened every day, displays a recklessness in the face of reality which is not only astounding, but also extremely reprehensible'.[41]

The 1974 resolution of the SACC not only challenged the very basis of the society which Pretoria was calling on young men to defend and if necessary die for, but it also suggested to blacks that any such defence would amount to an unjust war. Mr Botha declared that his government was 'after the blood of those persons who, wrapped in a cloak of santimoniousness, are trying to prejudice the security of South Africa'.[42] From that time onward police harassment and surveillance of the SACC and, finally, the Eloff commission looking into its working and financial affairs in 1982, showed that he meant it.

In the meantime the state oiled its propaganda apparatus and generated a war psychosis with renewed vigour. The authorities also started to refute the charges that apartheid society was fundamentally unjust. Thus, three months after the South African invasion of Angola and just one month before the outbreak of the 1976 uprising, P.W. Botha, in all sincerity, remarked: 'But in recent times there have been cunning attempts to discredit the SA Defence Force. One of the arguments advanced is the following one: "How can you expect people to fight for an unjust society like South Africa?" However, when we examine the matter closely, the question arises: Where in the world is there a more just society today than South Africa?'[43] Within

38. *Hansard*, August 1970, col. 2851.
39. Dr Morrison is the current deputy Minister of Co-operation and Development ('Bantu Administration') in the Botha government.
40. *Hansard*, 1 March 1972, col. 2246.
41. *Hansard*, 1 March 1972, col. 2247.
42. *Hansard*, 15 August 1974, col. 802.
43. *Hansard*, 6 May 1976, col. 6206.

two months SADF army units entered black townships around the country and over the next few months, in a major combined operation, para-military police left over 600 black people (mainly children) dead, thousands wounded, hundreds detained and many banned. By the end of 1977, with the murder of Steve Biko in detention and the banning of 18 black organisations and newspapers, it was becoming increasingly difficult to convince anyone that South African society was not unjust.

In the late 1970s the growing power of the military in government eroded the central institutions of white parliamentary politics. There was little evidence that the SADF was comparable with armies in countries committed to civilian parliamentary systems and liberal values, and General Malan admitted as much. 'There is a conflicting requirement between that of total strategy and the democratic system of government', he said in 1977.[44] Even more disconcerting was Malan's blunt acknowledgement two years later that the SADF supported the apartheid policy of a particular political party. 'The Defence Force supports government policy and is responsible for peace, law and order in this country. This policy is the same as that laid down by Dr H.F. Verwoerd, namely multinationalism and self-determination of nations'.[45] Liberals around the country were outraged. Malan had admitted the obvious, yet they refused to accept this. Surely the military should continue its pretence by maintaining the avowed neutral stance of the armed forces in all liberal democracies of the 'free world'.

In September 1979 the SADF, in a statement issued with the approval of P.W. Botha (then Prime Minister as well as Minister of Defence), completely dissociated itself from the attempts of the Cape Town pacifist group to establish an ambulance service as an alternative non-military form of national service.[46] Two weeks later deputy Defence Minister Coetsee said that the movement to establish a non-military service corps created a wonderful opportunity for others to abuse it so as not to do their duty. He said, 'Young men and soldiers hide behind theological and political principles, and the movement gives each coward and rotter a sanctuary where he could evade his responsibilities towards his country'.[47] According to Coetsee the Defence Force would under no circumstances allow its enemies to

---

44. Quoted by the then leader of the Progressive Federal Party, Colin W. Eglin, *Hansard*, 22 April 1977, col. 5897.
45. Quoted in the editorial of *The Cape Times*, 25 October 1979.
46. SABC, Internal English Service, 11.15h GMT, 15 September 1979; *The Sunday Times*, 16 September 1979.
47. *The Cape Times*, 2 October 1979. See also Coatsee's condemnation in SATV Newscast, 18.00h GMT, 28 September 1979.

proceed with their interference. Conscientious objection was occupying a growing part of state propaganda.

In February 1980 Prime Minister Botha hit out strongly at what he described as attempts to discourage young people from doing military service and not to fight for South Africa. He asked just what sort of just society there would be if the 'communists' succeeded in their aim of taking over the country. 'That is what we are fighting against', said Botha. He also asked where in the world there was greater freedom of religion, a more independent judiciary, greater press freedom and more 'free' enterprise than in South Africa.[48]

Articles in a similar vein began to appear in *Paratus*, the official journal of the SADF. These were initiated with a major focus on war resistance in March 1980. The Chaplain General of the SADF, Major General J.A. van Zyl, set out his views on conscientious objection. It is worth illustrating these in detail as they give an idea of the way in which a section of the church had been successfully co-opted by the military in its attempt to negate the support of church hierarchies for the right of conscientious objection.

Van Zyl began by acknowledging that 'Every Christian has the right to regulate his life according to the word of God'. With regard to the specific issue of conscientious objection he raised a number of questions such as: 'Is the Word of God ambiguous, in other words does it lead to conscientious objection for one person, while for another it is a call to responsibility — a God-given assignment to defend his country, his nation, his church, women and children and Christian civilisation?' and: 'Are some churches not opening the door for young men who wish to evade their responsibilities to do so under the cloak of conscientious objection?' He argued that while every sincere and faithful Christian has the right to act according to the word of God, God is not a capricious being who leads men and churches according to different standards. He went on to propound a pure version of the national security heresy. South Africa, he maintained, is a Christian society and for this reason it is the state's duty and privilege to ensure that Christian principles are protected. He intimated that the war in which South Africa is involved is a conflict between Christian principles and Marxism. He concluded:

> It is a question to be asked to those who defend the right of conscientious objection, if they are not playing into the hands of these Marxist powers by way of indirect support. They must also remember that it has been shown over and over again that those who have conscientious objections against Communism or Marxism and then

---

48. *The Natal Mercury*, Durban, 7 February 1980.

express those objections in those states, end up in punishment camps or gaols. This is what our Defence Force is fighting to defend us from!'[49]

In the same issue of *Paratus* spokesmen on defence matters from each of the three then existing opposition political parties in the white parliament, expressed their views on war resistance. All agreed that military service in the SADF was a duty from which no one should be excused on the grounds of conscientious objection. Since then articles on the justness of the SADF's cause have been regularly featured in *Paratus*. By the end of 1982 military leaders were talking on campuses, warning of the snares of conscientious objection.

The Current Situation

Evidence of the church's current determination to avoid any compromise of the Christian faith in the face of state hostility came in the form of a number of resolutions passed at the annual denominational meetings in the latter half of 1980. Typical of the new mood was a commitment by some 200 representative lay and clergy leaders of the Catholic Church, who met in early September in a unique inter-diocesan pastoral consultation to work for the 'total liberation' of all the peoples of southern Africa. Amongst a number of specific proposals, the meeting recommended that the Catholic bishops should establish a body which, *inter alia*, should give public support to conscientious objectors who refuse to render military forms of national service. At a press conference held after the meeting Archbishop Hurley explained that this recommendation could push the Catholic Church into adopting stands which are illegal in South Africa.[50]

In the following months the Presbyterian Church again included war resistance on its agenda,[51] while the Methodist Church resolved that any Methodist who, as a conscientious objector, refused to render military service, should receive the same treatment as members of the 'peace churches'.[52] But perhaps the most noteworthy development was the nationwide spate of protest resignations from the white NGK. Some of the main reasons given for the walkouts, which involved mainly professional people, was the NGK's refusal to criticise the government, its support for the political status quo and its 'blind backing' of the state's stand on conscientious objection.[53]

---

49. *Paratus*, March 1980, p.37.
50. *The Post*, Johannesburg, 3 September 1980; *The Star*, 6 September 1980.
51. *Rand Daily Mail*, 20 October 1980.
52. *Rand Daily Mail*, 24 October 1980.
53. *Cape Times*, 17 September 1980.

In 1980 the churches also took stands on wider issues relating to the SADF, apartheid militarisation and the developing liberation struggle in South Africa. In May the SACC conference called for support for war resisters and made a clear distinction between violence 'which is executed in pursuance of a just society' and the violence of the apartheid military state. In August, Prime Minister Botha refused to talk to the SACC until — amongst other things — they had dissociated themselves from 'undermining military service'. In October he demanded that the SACC visit the military operational area. The SACC refused.

Church-state relations then took a turn for the worse, with the churches increasingly taking options for the oppressed majority and taking a firm stand against apartheid and the government's 'total strategy'. The confrontation was at its sharpest over the 20th anniversary of the proclamation of South Africa as a republic. All the major denominations — except, most importantly, the Afrikaans churches — boycotted the celebrations of 20 years of apartheid and supported the call for a non-racial and democratic South Africa. It was not surprising that the issue of the military raised itself in this context. In Durban, the centre of the celebrations, there were military march-pasts, a full-scale amphibious landing was made on the beach, and military aircraft flew low over the city. In protest, many churches held services to coincide with the military parades. In one service, the Anglican Archbishop-elect, Philip Russell, warned that those who lived by the sword would die by the sword, and went on to pray for those who had defied the apartheid military system, like the Anglican war resister Charles Yeats.

Throughout 1981 the churches spoke out against state militarism, and for the first time there was some public condemnation in South Africa of SADF attacks on neighbouring countries. In February the SACC organised a service for the ANC members killed by the SADF in an attack on exile residences in Matola, Mozambique. In May a report tabled by the Justice and Reconciliation Division of the SACC to its annual congress warned that South Africa was already in a war situation because 'the South African government is resolved to maintain the present power structure by military force. At the same time the increasing number of attacks on strategic targets within the country is an indication that the liberation movements are resolved not to be intimidated by the numerical and technological superiority of the SADF'. This warning was repeated in May by the acting president of the SACC, Peter Storey, who pointed out that the greatest threat to peace and stability in South Africa was not the 'total onslaught' of government propaganda, but apartheid itself.

Perhaps the most daring affront to the national security state, however, came from the Anglican diocese of Kimberley and Kuruman in the Cape province, whose synod meeting in September discussed several motions including support for conscientious objectors. Other motions urged Anglicans not to buy Defence Force bonds, and requested the diocese to apply for exemption from tax payments because 'a major part of tax monies are used for the implementation of apartheid and the perpetuation of war on the borders of this country'.

Church-state conflict

In September, the Minister of Police, Mr le Grange, accused the SACC of supporting 'subversion' and encouraging 'a revolutionary climate'. Some of these 'subversive' activities, alleged Mr le Grange, included support for war resisters. Le Grange went on to accuse the SACC of working with banned liberation movements.

In reply to the Minister's accusations on war resistance, the acting president of the SACC, Peter Storey, declared:

> Let me make it absolutely clear that so long as the rights of people who, in conscience, refuse to take arms are not respected by the Government of the Republic of South Africa, so long will the churches fight for those rights. We do not believe that any Government on earth has the right to conscript a man's conscience. Within our member churches there is an honourable tradition which has always been respected by those churches (it may not have been shared by everybody in those churches) of respecting and fighting for the right of anybody who says 'In obedience to Jesus Christ, I cannot take up a weapon against my fellowman'. We are not ashamed of that position. It is the Government who should be ashamed, for it has made it very difficult for people who hold that conscientious position.
>
> I think it is a disgrace that there are people of high principle and great courage who are languishing in prison, who have simply said 'Under God I cannot kill another man'. That may be the ultimate obedience to Jesus Christ.

The church-state conflict was heightened in October by the adoption of a resolution at the Presbyterian Assembly calling for disobedience to unjust apartheid laws; a motion which obviously had a bearing on the right to conscientious objection. This motion — which also urged ministers to defy the law and marry people of different races — was supported by the Anglican, Catholic and Methodist churches. The Methodist Conference went further, urging Methodists to 'take the struggle against apartheid into every home'. The Methodist Conference also spoke out against the state's militarism, and the secretary of the church's Christian Education and

Youth Department pointed out that young whites seemed to be encouraged to 'kill as many people as possible'.

The debate on war resistance was given new impetus by the repeated conviction and incarceration of Charles Yeats, an official in the Anglican Church who refused to render military service on pacifist and political grounds. He was convicted in May 1981 and once in Detention Barracks was required to wear the regulation military dress and perform military drill. This he refused to do. As a result he was ordered to remove his civilian clothes with the threat that they would be removed with force if he did not. After spending a few days in Detention Barracks in nothing but shorts, Yeats petitioned the Supreme Court for an order to have his civilian clothes returned. Pending the court's decision the Detention Barracks authorities agreed to permit him to wear a pair of blue 'conscientious objector' overalls. The SADF representative informed the court that no concession could be made and that the reprieve given to Moll and Steele the year before was a 'fatal error'.[54] The court rejected Yeats' plea and after periods in solitary confinement had failed to break his resolve he was 'ignominiously discharged' from the SADF and sentenced in December 1981 to one year in a civilian prison for refusal to obey a 'lawful command', to wear regulation brown military overalls. This strange tactic got Yeats out of the limelight by giving him a 'dishonourable discharge' without conceding to him on any points of principle.

Yeats' first conviction came under strong criticism from church leaders. In a statement nine clergymen, including Archbishops Hurley and Burnett, expressed great concern at the sentence, and continued: 'We urge the government to understand that in the circumstances, conscientious objection can be based on genuine religious and moral convictions. We urge the government to regularise the position of conscientious objectors'. They added again a call for alternative non-military forms of national service and requested the government to exercise towards people like Yeats the humanity that should be characteristic of a Christian society. A number of other ministers also criticised the sentence.[55] After the December 1981 sentence the new Anglican Archbishop of Cape Town, Russell, declared that it had been South Africa on trial, not Yeats.

In March 1982 another Baptist, Michael Viveiros, 24, was discharged and sentenced to 18 months in a civilian prison for refusing military call up on the grounds that 'I would be required to defend the present system, a result of apartheid ideology, which is contrary to all

---

54. *Rand Daily Mail*, 8 August 1981.
55. *Rand Daily Mail*, 14 May 1981.

the teachings of Jesus Christ'. The state made it clear that on his release he could be called up again and face further imprisonment. After the sentence, the president of the SACBC, Archbishop Hurley, expressed his admiration for Viveiros' stand and his 'dismay' that the military courts still imposed punitive sentences on war resisters. Significantly, both Viveiros and Yeats are held in Pretoria Central Prison, where most white political prisoners are detained.

Later in June Neil Mitchell became the first Roman Catholic to pay for his opposition to military service with a year's sentence to military detention barracks. 'I would be required to go along with the dehumanisation of the enemy into people to be hated, thereby denying their human dignity', he declared to the military court. The Catholic military ordinary, Archbishop George Daniel of Pretoria, supported his stand and called for an alternative form of non-military service to cater for those whose conscience dictated a pacifist position. A secondary school teacher and universal pacifist, Neil Mitchell was repeatedly subjected to solitary confinement for refusing to wear brown military overalls, before being sent to a civilian prison.

Collision course

There is every indication today that the implications of the struggle over military service between the churches and the state are not lost on either side. The churches are now attempting, through conferences and education programmes, to alert Christians to the issue of conscience involved in bearing arms in an apartheid society. Efforts are being made to create national structures embodying their teaching on conscientious objection.

The state in turn is determined to oppose the spread of the war resistance movement, to press on with militarisation, and to minimise the publicity value of courageous imprisoned Christians. Structures and legislation to carry out this programme are already being laid down.

In early 1982 the South African Army Non-Effective Troops Section (SAANETS) was set up to monitor young people with deferments and, although this is denied, to persecute war resisters. This special section was created in direct response to the success of the war resistance movement. Spokesmen for SAANETS boast 'We always get our man', and the section is designed to deal with university students and others whose political views would make them suspect to the South African authorities. This focus on South African universities is motivated by the growing discussion of war resistance on the campuses, particularly those of the Universities of Cape Town and Witwatersrand, where major forums on the topic were held during 1982.

Legislation is also being passed to extend service in the Citizen Force from eight years, 240 days, to 12 years, 720 days.[56] This will take the form of a maximum of 120 days' service in any two-year period. Some form of military service will be required of white males from the age of 17 until 55 years of age. This extension of service was motivated by the failure of the volunteer commando units, which, according to the SADF,[57] were 37% undermanned. South Africans were refusing to volunteer for commando duties, and national servicemen were filling the gap.[58] Now there will be compulsory service in local commandos with a maximum 50-day period per year up to 1 000 days, and conscription of immigrants is likely. Given the military needs of the white minority faced with a violent equilibrium between state repression and growing black revolt, the churches are obviously on a collision course with the government over the issue of conscientious objection. It is probable that the government may concede, under pressure, a two- to four-year period of non-military service for 'religious' objectors. This would enable government conveniently to divide the war resister movement by making concessions to Christian objectors while leaving 'secular' or humanist objectors subject to detention. This would resolve an immediate issue, but the underlying conflict would remain. Even if such concessions were to be made, they would still not satisfy those with political objections to serving the apartheid state in any way, or those with religious objections to state service like the Jehovah's Witnesses. The state would go on demanding conscripts. The churches would continue to question the justice of defending an unjust society.

56. *Rand Daily Mail*, 24 March 1982.
57. ibid.
58. ibid.

4. Military Chaplains

Since the introduction of universal conscription for white males in 1967 the military authorities have sought to assert greater control over clergymen in the armed forces. Within the SADF there is a special Chaplains' Corps which includes clergymen from the Permanent Force as well as those who are conscripted for service in the Citizen Force and Commandos.

Clergymen are not exempted from compulsory military service by virtue of their office. In addition, there are a number of civilian chaplains who minister to military servicemen on a part-time basis. All full-time military chaplains are members of the SADF, are paid by the SADF and are subject to military discipline. They carry military rank and receive the pay that goes with it. They are required to undergo military training including combat training with weapons. From 1971 they received their training and orientation at the South African Army College at Voortrekkerhoogte and since May 1976 at the Chaplains Training Centre which operates as an autonomous unit of the Army College. The head of the Chaplains' Corps is the Chaplain General, currently Major General J.A. van Zyl.

The role of the military chaplain is succinctly summed up in the insignia of the Chaplains' Corps. These consist of a cross with the inscription 'In hoc signo' which conjures up images of the mediaeval crusades and finds its inspiration in the legend of the Roman Emperor Constantine's vision of a cross before battle: 'In this sign you will conquer'. The task of the military chaplain is to instil this vision in the mind of every SADF soldier, whether he be sweating on a dusty parade ground, bombing economic installations in Angola or shooting children in Soweto. Chaplain General Van Zyl insists that the church cannot detach itself from the struggle of the SADF,[1] and in his 1979

---

1. *Paratus*, Vol.30, No.4, April 1979, p.23.

Christmas message he described this struggle as follows: '. . . our Defence Force serves the Christ of Christmas and takes up arms to defend this Christmas patron — this is what it is all about, because this is what we are fighting for'.[2]

Van Zyl came to the following conclusion about war resistance: 'Therefore in this time no conscientious objector and no pacifist can kneel before the crib of Bethlehem with a clean conscience. How can he enjoy Christian freedom without defending Christ and his message?'[3]

These are typical of the views which in large part determine the direction of the Chaplains' Corps. For, as Van Zyl told chaplain conscripts at a parade earlier in 1979, by being with the soldiers in the military base or on the 'border', 'you can make a contribution to ensure the continued existence of the Christian religion in South Africa'.[4]

The Challenge to the Role of Chaplains

The role of military chaplains was first seriously challenged by the churches in the 1974 SACC resolution in which the SACC National Conference called 'on those of its member churches who have Chaplains in the military forces to reconsider the basis on which they are appointed and to investigate the state of pastoral care available to the communicants at present in exile or under arms beyond our borders and to seek ways and means of ensuring that such pastoral care may be properly exercised'.

The issue was not taken up again until January 1976, and in the particular context of Namibia, in the wake of the South African invasion of Angola, when Colin Winter, then Anglican Bishop-in-exile of Namibia, forbade the Dean of Windhoek and the Archdeacon of Walvis Bay to act as honorary chaplains to the SADF. The Archbishop of Cape Town, Bill Burnett, disagreed with this position, but added that the church should minister to all, including those fighting on the other side of the borders.[5]

In May 1976, at a consultation prior to the SACC National Conference of that year, the following statement was issued: 'Black Christians call on all churches in South Africa to withdraw recognition of chaplains appointed and paid by the SADF, and to make their own independent arrangements for pastoral care of all

2. *Paratus*, Vol.30, No.12, December 1979, p.3.
3. ibid.
4. *Paratus*, Vol.30, No.4, April 1979, p.23.
5. *EcuNews*, 21 January 1976.

persons involved in armed struggle on both sides of the border'.[6] Again it was in the more democratic Methodist Church, where the voice of black Christians was strongest, that the issue came to prominence. At the annual conference of the MCSA in October 1976, Rev. Peter Storey moved a motion calling on his church, in conjunction with other denominations, to renegotiate the status of military chaplains with the SADF. There was also a concerted effort, led by Rev. Ernest Baartman, to persuade the denomination to withdraw its chaplains from the SADF unless they could also serve men 'on the other side of the border'. Mr Baartman argued that every country must have a defence force, but that the SADF was not viewed by blacks as necessarily protecting their interests. An ex-chaplain in the SADF, Rev. Arthur Attwell, told the conference that he had left the SADF because he could no longer identify with 'the system'.[7]

At the same time Rev. Brian Brown wrote an open letter to Methodist chaplains in the SADF, raising a number of crucial issues:

Dear Brethren,

As pastors engaged in preparing young men for participation in the SADF, I would value your answers to the questions which follow. Your response will help me, and possibly other clergy, to determine to what degree one can encourage potential combatants to discuss these vital matters with their Methodist chaplains.

I have personally presented the questions to one of our senior chaplains and expressed my desire to publicise the answers so as to create as much awareness as possible.

1. Does the Methodist Church of South Africa and/or its military chaplains believe that its members may participate in any war or only in a just war?
2. Did the Angolan war, and, more specifically, the participation of the SADF in it, meet the conditions of a just war?
3. Did the Methodist chaplains inform the men under their pastoral care that the then relevant section 95(1)(a) of the Defence Act of 1957 allowed them to refuse to serve in Angola? If not, why not?
4. Do our Methodist chaplains consider it essential to point out to the men under their care any difference between a war waged within our borders and a war on foreign soil?
5. Do the Methodist chaplains include the following topics in their pastoral teaching or in their preaching:
   a. the church's teaching about a just war?
   b. the four Geneva Conventions of 1949?
   c. the International Committee of the Red Cross Draft Rules for the Limitations of the Dangers incurred by the Civilian Population in Time of War?'

6. *EcuNews*, 26 May 1976.
7. *EcuNews*, 29 October 1976.

Not surprisingly, the Superintendent of the SADF Circuit replied, 'In regard to the questions posed by Mr Brown, we have no intention of permitting ourselves to be drawn into a public debate on them'.[8] Nevertheless, the Methodist Church adopted a set of guidelines on military chaplains designed to reduce their identification with the military. Among other things the Methodists requested that all chaplains have civilian status and proposed that a pool of ministers be selected and, after suitable SADF screening, sent to the 'operational area' on a roster basis for limited periods. The SADF would pay such chaplains during their service.[9] Soon after the Catholic Bishops, meeting in the annual session of the SACBC in February 1978, decided to accept the Methodist guidelines as a basis for renegotiating the status of chaplains in the SADF to reduce their identification with the military.[10] In response the Chaplain General of the SADF let it be known that he would reply to any request made to him by the Catholic bishops that chaplains be 'demilitarised'.[11]

The move to alter the status of military chaplains suffered a serious setback when, on 1 March 1978, a meeting of all Permanent Force chaplains from the English-language denominations in the SADF unanimously decided that, although being in uniform had some disadvantages, given that 'some SADF members might prefer a civilian minister to a man in uniform and also that strong feelings do exist among certain sections of the population that chaplains in uniform are identified with the Defence Force which appears to them to be the armed agent of the political party in power . . . the uniformed chaplain performs the more effective ministry'. They strongly recommended that 'the status quo be maintained'.[12]

Within the Methodist Church itself there were some fierce reactions to the stand of the National Conference on the chaplaincy question. These came from conservative quarters, as in June 1978, when the annual synod of the white-dominated Cape of Good Hope District adopted several resolutions supporting the concept of uniformed chaplains and calling on the church to resist any moves to withdraw them. The President of the Women's Auxiliary, Mrs D. Hittler, said that the mothers and wives of the men serving in the SADF honoured the work of the chaplains and that the spiritual help needed by these men could best be given by chaplains who were members of the SADF rather than by civilian chaplains who would, in

8. *Pro Veritate*, October 1976.
9. *The Cape Times*, 28 February 1978.
10. *The Cape Times*, 9 February 1978.
11. *The Cape Times*, 28 February 1978.
12. *EcuNews*, 31 March 1978; *The Citizen*, Johannesburg, 14 March 1978; *Paratus* Supplement, May 1978.

many respects, be outsiders. At the same time Rev. E. Hymer of Rosebank, a full-time military chaplain for many years, criticised the National Conference for adopting a controversial stand on the matter without referring it to the opinion and feelings of the church as a whole. He said that Methodist chaplains had been offended and possibly insulted by much of the discussions within the church on their status.[13]

In October 1978 the subject of military chaplains again came up for discussion at the National Conference of the MCSA. It was resolved that all chaplains would have to obtain the nomination of the President of the Conference before they could be accepted as military chaplains within the SADF. However, the Conference also modified its stance in a resolution which declared 'its belief that chaplains appointed to serve in the South African Defence Force are able to exercise a full and effective ministry within the military context, and further declares its conviction that no chaplain serving within this context need feel that his presence in the Defence Force indicates moral support for the policy pursued by the Government which may be in power'.[14]

After this attempt to appease the SADF chaplains the Conference declared 'its disapproval of conscripting Ministers and Ministers in training for military service, believing that Ministers should be permitted to volunteer or not for military service according to their Christian convictions'. The Conference also insisted 'that so long as Ministers of the Methodist Church continue to be conscripted for National military service, they be not required to bear arms or be trained for combat'.[15]

Ministry to guerrilla forces

The 1978 Methodist National Conference also marked the emergence of a new emphasis on the issue of military chaplains. While the Conference decided 'to continue, under the existing conditions, its ministry with the SADF', it also resolved 'to undertake positive steps, during the ensuing year, to share as far as possible with churches in neighbouring states in providing effective ministry to Methodists serving as freedom fighters'.[16] Faced with strong opposition from its largely conservative white membership, its own military chaplains and the state, the Methodist hierarchy in practice decided to drop its effort

---

13. *The Star*, 17 June 1978.
14. Minutes of the 96th Annual Conference of the Methodist Church of South Africa, East London, October 1978, p.194.
15. ibid.
16. ibid., p.196.

to 'demilitarise' its chaplaincy in the SADF. Yet, because of the increasingly powerful voice of its progressive constituents and the establishment of a strong black caucus, it could not relinquish its responsibility entirely and therefore opted for an apparently indisputable traditional Christian position to minister neutrally to both sides in the conflict. Even the SADF and the white NGK conceded the theoretical legitimacy of this position.

This strategy had been adopted in other major denominations outside South Africa. The Anglican Diocese in Namibia established a Christian presence in camps of the South West African People's Organisation (SWAPO) and had two chaplains working amongst SWAPO exiles in Zambia.[17] In September 1980 the church leaders present at the Catholic inter-diocesan pastoral consultation recommended that the Catholic bishops should establish a body which would develop ways of advising and giving pastoral care to 'those who are drawn into the armed struggle', including persons on both sides of the conflict.[18] A year later stormy meetings between representatives of the Catholic Church in Namibia and SADF Catholic Chaplains took place. The Namibian church representatives made it clear that they regarded the SADF as an army of occupation and that they were unwilling to minister to it in any way.

However, the Methodists' 1978 initiatives never got off the ground. No response was received when the MCSA wrote to Methodist authorities in Angola and Zambia to establish the need for chaplains. Undeterred, the Methodist hierarchy pressed on in its efforts to find a solution to the chaplaincy question, and began a limited restructuring of the Methodist chaplaincy in the SADF. The Methodists withdrew from the United Board of Free Churches, a joint body which provided chaplains to Baptist, Presbyterian, Congregational and Methodist members, and took over direct control of their chaplaincy system in the SADF. Then at its annual Conference in October 1980 the subject of military chaplains was once again placed on the agenda. After some debate the Conference decided to extend its military chaplain service to Methodists in 'guerrilla forces' outside the country. The MCSA also agreed to accept financial responsibility for posting such chaplains outside the country. Finally, a call was made for Methodist ministers to volunteer as chaplains to the guerrilla forces.[19]

17. *The Star*, 25 October 1980; Interview with Fr Ed Morrow, Anglican Vicar General of Namibia until his deportation, 1978. The Lutherans also provided chaplains.
18. *The Post*, 3 September 1980; *The Star*, 6 September 1980.
19. *The Cape Times*, 23 October 1980; *Rand Daily Mail*, 23 October 1980; *The Star*, 25 October 1980.

In response a spokesman for the SADF Chaplain General said at the conference that the SADF still had no objection to chaplains ministering to both sides in a conflict situation. But he stressed that if a minister wished to cross the border from the 'operational area' to preach to guerrillas, he would have to obtain a letter from his denomination relieving the SADF of responsibility for his safety and for caring for his family should he be killed.[20]

However, the issue remained an important one for many black Christians, and black concern about the failure of the churches to implement the proposed ministry to freedom fighters was expressed in a resolution passed by the SACC executive in March 1981, which requested the General Secretary to find out what progress had been made in member churches, with 'a view to mobilising the support of chaplains' for this task. Three months later, at a press conference to protest at the detention of an SACC worker who was collecting information on the needs of refugees in surrounding states, the SACC reaffirmed its commitment to 'minister on both sides'. It was also announced that a consultation on ministry to refugees — which included 'forces in conflict with the SADF' — was in progress. The Methodist, Anglican and Catholic churches were represented. Later in the year the Methodist Church again decided at its annual conference to approach churches in neighbouring countries with a view to offering 'spiritual care to South African exiles, including those 'fighting on the other side of the border'. A plan to circulate a letter to ministers calling for volunteers for this duty was dropped after legal advisers had warned that it could constitute an offence under security legislation.

For the moment the Methodist decision has set the direction for several churches on the question of military chaplains. But it represents an uneasy compromise between the majority in the church on the one hand, and the state and conservative church members on the other. It is a compromise which cannot be maintained for much longer. For the church cannot afford to remain in a position where it provides spiritual inspiration for the goals and hopes of both sides locked in an increasingly vicious and violent conflict. If it does, it risks rejection by both sides and renders the gospel contentless and directionless. While not identifying uncritically with any political faction, the churches must retain the right to pronounce on the justice of a cause and express this judgement in concrete options. The church cannot and must not seek a 'third way' reconciling oppressor and oppressed, without removing oppression.

---

20. *The Cape Times*, 23 October 1980; *The Star*, 25 October 1980.

5. Into the Future

The churches' opposition to the militarisation of South African society, their support of the right to object to military service on conscientious grounds, and the insistence of some on ministering to the liberation armies have made an important contribution to the widening rift between churches and the apartheid regime. But more important, these developments have been part of a growing church commitment to liberation in South and southern Africa and the increased militancy with which the church is currently pursuing this aim.

The lead has come from those parts of the Christian community where change has been permitted to take place by pressure from below, from the black majority and committed radical whites. In this respect the SACC has been the leading organisation within South Africa. It demonstrated this quite dramatically in 1980 when its national conference challenged the various denominations to encourage and support non-violent civil disobedience in opposition to the apartheid regime. Again the Methodist Church, with its democratic structures which permitted the black voice to be heard was the one which took the lead when, in October 1981, its national conference came out clearly in support of a free and undivided South Africa, took uncompromising stands on apartheid, which it described as a 'disease', and committed the church to breaking down racial barriers and engaging in social action.

The year before, the conference had aligned itself with the aims of strikes and school boycotts and resolved to support individuals who resorted to civil disobedience 'wherever appropriate'.[1] There is growing pressure in the other denominations for the adoption of a similar approach. Youth groups in both the Anglican and Catholic communions have, by acting with considerable restraint and maturity, begun to see their views on war resistance take purchase in their respective hierarchies.

---

1. *Rand Daily Mail*, 24 October 1980; *The Cape Times*, 23 October 1980.

These activities have led to an intensification of attacks by the state on the church. Public rows between church leaders and cabinet ministers are occurring more frequently and the church has come to learn that no protection against bannings, arrests and detention will be afforded to ministers. In the latter half of 1980 talks were held between the government and the SACC in a vain attempt at 'reconciliation'. Perhaps the only positive lesson which emerged from this exercise was the realisation by church leaders that the church and state are indeed poles apart, and that no amount of talking is going to bring them closer together unless it is accompanied by fundamental change amounting to the eradication of the apartheid system and not merely its amendment.

The inevitable church-state confrontation in South Africa will doubtless provide a spur to a more profound process, creating a genuinely South African church ready to take the side of the poor and oppressed in practical action. The issues associated with military service have illuminated the need in the churches for the development of a biblically rooted political theology and ethics. The Jesus witnessed to by church hierarchies has, on the whole, been a liberal champion of individual choice rather than the servant of a people, suffering for his partisan attacks on the socio-religious system of the day, an ahistorical moral judge, rather than the Lord of history.

The fundamental issues of Christian approaches to violence and to justice in a South African context are only now being given a firm theological framework in which the issue of conscientious objection would find a natural place. Because underlying questions have only recently begun to arise, with small groups in the churches acting as pathfinders, the question of war resistance has sometimes risked generating more heat than light.

The vexing question of military chaplains is a symptom of this past lack of an adequate theological framework. Whatever may be said in their justification, however much the churches must provide a ministry to all people, military chaplains symbolise the Christian legitimation of the South African military and its role. The problem posed by such chaplains has, in a sense, been evaded dishonestly. The provision of chaplains for freedom fighters — and these have come exclusively from the Namibian churches — avoids coming to grips with fundamental problems: how can the churches be neutral in the face of institutionalised violence, sometimes condemned openly, and the subsequent violent response of the oppressed, more often formally condemned in blanket rejections of violence by the churches? The Namibian churches have been significantly less 'neutral' than the South African churches until recently. At a 1982 meeting of the Cape Town synod of the Anglican Church considerable pressure was put on military chaplains to explain on what moral grounds they performed their duties.

For most church hierarchies the burning question of wars of liberation has in practice been split into Christian statements about an abstract concept of war and an abstract liberation. The wars in southern Africa today, however, are not comparable with the medieval assemblies of clashing soldiers in which the churches' teaching on war originated, or with the territorial conflicts of nation states. In both of these the churches might legitimately find no moral issue, save the violence, which they duly deplored. The present wars in southern Africa, however, as the churches are belatedly coming to realise, turn on a very clear moral issue, and the churches are being forced to admit, with more or less reluctance, that justice is fundamentally on one side, that of the black majority. Similarly in South Africa, abstract commitments to liberation are being tested by the existence of actual liberation movements with detailed strategies for bringing liberation about.

The churches therefore find themselves uncomfortably poised between a Christian universal pacifist tradition, just war theories which admit the possibility of war under certain conditions but with a calculus of suffering that is difficult, if not impossible to measure, and traditions of opposition to tyranny which allow insurrection when all peaceful methods have failed. Pitted against them is the National Party and the military forces of South Africa's white minority for whom the battle in southern Africa is against communism. Though this may often be seriously believed, it more often has the character of a legitimation for repression and aggression.

Ironically, the claim of the South African Chaplain General is exactly the claim of the Crusaders: we fight for the salvation of Christendom. This claim, which is essentially an heretical identification of the apartheid system with the Christian moral order, defines the issue of militarism in South Africa as one on which neutrality is not permissible. Militarism in the South African context is not only a grave deformation of civil society, and therefore profoundly anti-Christian, but the means to perpetuate a particular Christian ideology which calls in question the teaching authority of the churches and their fidelity to the gospel.

To take sides in such a conflict is a theological and ideological choice. Making such choices defines what Christianity is all about. This is the function of church leaders, even if they are the last to wish to perform it, valuing as they do the unity of the church. However this unity, as the expulsion of the white Reformed Church in South Africa from communion with the world reformed tradition recently demonstrated, cannot be maintained at the expense of truth.

In the South African context, taking sides will not mean abandoning the right of individual choice, based on conscience, in favour of a spurious situation ethics. On the contrary, the spirituality growing out of a biblically rooted theology will reinforce and inform individual choice by making it the choice of a community in struggle for a genuinely Christian vision of society. Nor will it push aside spiritual concerns in favour of secular political action; rather we find a renewed spirituality growing out of the concrete world of prisons, Detention Barracks, exile, police harassment and communal efforts to plan an exodus from the captivity of apartheid. This spirituality has a claim to be closer to the New Testament, for it admits a Jesus who is angry with the oppressor, divides mother from son and speaks of genuine enemies, who yet, as individuals, are to be loved.

For the churches in South Africa and their leaders, the 1980s have become a time to choose, and this choice will undoubtedly identify the fight against militarism as a primary task. The court-martial in October 1982 of an Anglican seminarian, William Paddock, who selectively objected to military service on the ground of a commitment to the liberation of South Africa, is further confirmation that white Christians are already making these difficult choices. His action posed in inescapable form the question of the fundamental illegitimacy of any service in the cause of apartheid. What remains to be seen is whether, in the face of the ruthless determination of the South African state, the churches can find the will, the theology, the spirituality and the strategies to prosecute their task effectively.

Appendix A

The 1974 Resolution of the South African Council of Churches

The National Conference of the SACC acknowledges as the one and only God him who mightily delivered the people of Israel from their bondage in Egypt and who in Jesus Christ still proclaims that He will 'set at liberty those who are oppressed' (Luke 4.18). He alone is supreme Lord and Saviour and to him alone we owe ultimate obedience. Therefore 'we must obey God rather than men' in those areas where the Government fails to fulfil its calling to be 'God's servant for good' rather than for evil and for oppression (Acts 5.29; Romans 13.4).

In the light of this the Conference:

1. Maintains that Christians are called to strive for justice and the true peace which can be founded only on justice;

2. does not accept that it is automatically the duty of those who follow Christ, the Prince of Peace, to engage in violence and war, or to prepare to engage in violence or war, whenever the state demands it;

3. reminds its member churches that both Catholic and Reformation theology has regarded the taking up of arms as justifiable, if at all, only in order to fight a 'just war';

4. points out that the theological definition of a 'just war' excludes war in defence of a basically unjust and discriminatory society;

5. points out that the Republic of South Africa is at present a fundamentally unjust and discriminatory society and that this injustice and discrimination constitutes the primary, institutionalised violence which has provoked the counter-violence of the terrorists or freedom fighters;

6. points out that the military forces of our country are being prepared to defend this unjust and discriminatory society and that the threat of military force is in fact already used to defend the status quo against moves for radical change from outside the white electorate;

7. maintains that it is hypocritical to deplore the violence of terrorists or freedom fighters while we ourselves prepare to defend our society with its primary, institutionalised violence by means of yet more violence;

8. points out further that the injustice and oppression under which the black peoples of South Africa labour is far worse than that against which Afrikaners waged their First and Second Wars of Independence and that if we

have justified the Afrikaners' resort to violence (or the violence of the imperialism of the English) or claimed that God was on their side, it is hypocritical to deny that the same applies to the black people in their struggle today;

9. questions the basis upon which chaplains are seconded to the military forces lest their presence indicate moral support for the defence of our unjust and discriminatory society;

The Conference therefore:

1. deplores violence as a means to solve problems;

2. calls on its member churches to challenge all their members to consider in view of the above whether Christ's call to take up the cross and follow him in identifying with the oppressed does not, in our situation, involve becoming conscientious objectors;

3. calls on those of its member churches who have chaplains in the military forces to reconsider the basis on which they are appointed and to investigate the state of pastoral care available to the communicants at present in exile under arms beyond our borders and to seek ways and means of ensuring that such pastoral care may be properly exercised;

4. commends the courage and witness of those who have been willing to go to jail in protest against unjust laws and policies in our land, and who challenge all of us by their example;

5. requests the SACC's task force on Violence and Non-violence to study methods of non-violent action for change which can be recommended to its member churches;

6. prays for the Government and people of our land and urgently calls on them to make rapid strides towards radical and peaceful change in our society so that the violence and war to which our social, economic and political policies are leading us may be avoided.

Appendix B

Statements from South African Christian Conscientious Objectors

Peter Moll

Excerpts from an open letter addressed to the Officer Commanding, Cape Flats Commando, 19 October 1979

Dear Sir,
CONSCIENTIOUS OBJECTION TO CONTINUOUS TRAINING CAMP
    I note that I am required to attend a training camp from 19 November to 7 December 1979. After much serious consideration and study, and after consulting my church leaders about the matter, I have come to the conclusion that to obey would be a grave moral compromise of my faith. *I therefore refuse to do so.* My explanation is as follows. (The first two points have been summarised.)

1. Pacifism
The Christian church has traditionally been concerned about involvement with the military, which means the taking of men's lives.

2. Civil disobedience
Christians obey the government, but reserve the right to disobey if obedience does not conform to their religious and moral convictions.

3. Selective conscientious objection
Selective conscientious objection is the refusal to engage in a particular war, while making no necessary statement about war in general. I have decided to be a selective conscientious objector because
    a. in terms of Christian moral standards. South African society is fundamentally unjust;
    b. the insurgents are generally not foreigners but South African citizens — i.e. the situation is one of civil war; and
    c. this makes one question very seriously just what one is required to fight for, and what one is required to die for. I shall devote one paragraph to each of these three points.
    In the Pentateuch we are commanded to protect the widow, the orphan,

the slave and the foreigner. The prophets castigated Israel for her oppression of the poor, for her unfair trading methods, and for the way the rich were favoured in the law and the courts. In the gospels we find Jesus urging us to break with Mammon (i.e. riches) once and for all. Paul urges us to do good to all men, and James rails at rich landowners who exploit their labourers. In South Africa we seem to find precisely the conditions which the biblical writers condemned so forcefully. Our land is one of vast inequalities — in wealth, in power and in education. White hegemony is guaranteed because they have taken to themselves 87% of the country's land area, leaving a meagre 13% for the larger part of the population. What is more, the so-called 'white homeland' has the lion's share of the country's mineral wealth. Migratory labour, which has been condemned by all the churches in the country, reinforces this skewed pattern of development, whereby some get rich at the expense of others. To keep it all intact there is that most hated aspect of a hated system, the pass laws, under which more than 1 000 people are being imprisoned daily. This is a situation of fundamental injustice. Until it is the government's express intention to remove it, I will be unable in conscience to defend it.

For decades blacks have tried to change matters by constitutional and peaceful means. Their attempts have been fruitless, because of the violent reprisals by the government of the day. Bannings, detentions without trial and shootings have removed all hope of peaceful change. Dare we be surprised if blacks turn to violent means? This is exactly what many have done. Those who go up to fight for the SADF on the border should remember that they are fighting against their own deeply disaffected fellow-citizens. They are taking part in a highly partisan civil war. It is as Lyndon Johnson said: Those who make pacific revolution impossible make violent revolution inevitable.

Young men are being required increasingly to risk their lives under arms. Many, like myself, are already asking: *Just what are we fighting for? Just what are we being required to die for?* Are we going to die for a better society, for a more just society, perhaps even for a more loving society? Are we *really* defending the last bastion of Christianity, as we are so often told? Is this that we are defending *really* to be termed 'civilisation', as against its alternative, 'barbarism', as again we are told by those who are left cold by the extraordinarily barbaric death of Steve Biko? There is a mockery in all of this. We fail to see that it is our own vices that are thrown back in our face by the revolutionary movements.

4. Churches support selective conscientious objection
There is a cloud of witnesses to support my understanding of the situation. Archbishop Denis Hurley (*Ecunews*, 11.9.74) said that 'the unjust situation in South Africa makes it justifiable for young South Africans to refuse to fight on the borders. It is our duty to discourage people from getting involved in this military conflict because of the realities of the South African situation — a situation of oppression'. Archbishop Bill Burnett said in 1975 that 'we need to grasp the significance of the fact that some black South Africans, many of whom are Christians, are outside our country seeking to change our power structure by force'. In March 1979 he said even more explicitly: 'Unless things

change significantly I would be unable in conscience to defend a system of government which, in spite of many good features, has a basis which is indefensible and produces fruit which is unjust and cruel.'

The Catholic bishops declare that 'we defend the right of every individual to follow his own conscience, the right therefore to conscientious objection both on the grounds of universal pacifism and on the grounds that he seriously believes the war to be unjust.' The Anglican Synod of Cape Town (1977) upheld the archbishop's statement that 'the society we have created for ourselves is morally indefensible. This is very serious at a time when we are being asked to defend it.' It went on: 'We sympathise with those who in conscience believe that it is an act of disobedience to God to be part of the military structures of this country because they are convinced that by doing so they would be defending what is morally indefensible. We accept that we, as a church, have a positive duty to make all people aware of what is involved in being used to defend the morally indefensible and to challenge each other in the cost of discipleship, putting first the claims of Christ over all our being and doing.'

In October 1979 the Baptist Union Assembly requested that the authorities provide a non-military alternative to military service for conscientious objectors. In September 1979 the Presbyterian Church affirmed solidarity of fellowship to any member of the church penalised following refusal to do military service. It insists that Christians had to reject as blasphemous a view that they should not venture into debate on bearing arms, the defence of the country or conscientious objection because of the risk of prosecution.

5. Rejection of non-combatant medical service in the unit

It is against this background that my refusal to attend the camp must be seen. I understand that I am required to be a medical officer in the unit from now on. In 1977, when I was a conscientious objector for the first time, I did not request non-combatant status but instead a 'period of service of national interest *under civilian direction*'. The latter phase is crucial. Being a medic does in no way absolve one from the serious moral compromise which I have explained above. A medic is a necessary part of the war machine; he too makes a direct contribution to the strength of the fighting force.

Therefore I find it impossible even to be a medical officer.

In the 1976 Parliamentary debate on the Defence Budget, J.J. Vilonel said, 'It would be ridiculous to argue about which division of the Defence Force is really the most important. The fact is that they are all important and that they are all essential. One important and essential division of the Defence Force is the Medical Corps. Not only does this corps play a vital role with regard to the health and physical preparedness of our men, but also with regard to the services it provides to the dependants, its welfare work and its role in regard to the wounded in wartime' (*Hansard*, 1976: cols 6243 and 6245). He has argued my case very well. If it is morally repugnant to be a fighting member of the SADF, then to be a medical officer is likewise problematic.

Richard Steele (*IFOR Report* **November 1981, 10-14**)

What led you toward refusing military service?
Whatever I was doing in my life I wanted to reflect my Christianity. In considering the issue of military service, which is obligatory in South Africa for men, I had to consider it in the light of Christian faith. Just in seeing who Jesus Christ is, someone absolutely gentle and caring and life-giving, you come to ask a simple question: Would he, if he received military call-up papers, go and do military service? My conclusion was that he wouldn't.

What was the response of friends to this?
I was told that I was being foolish and that it was my Christian duty to go into the military.

Foolish?
Foolish both from a religious and practical point of view. They thought going to prison was an absolute waste of time.

No doubt there were those who advised Jesus that getting crucified would be a waste of time.
Quite right. It is extraordinary how people react just to the possibility of going to prison, not remembering how Christ was treated as a common criminal.

Yet at some point it must have hit you with enormous force that there were alternatives. What about non-combatant service within the military?
That is an option, and it was re-opened even after I had gone to prison. There were several offers. 'We have made special arrangements,' one officer said, 'to have you assigned to work as a clerk in the office of a military chaplain. You won't have to do any basic training. No weapons. No marching. Just put on the uniform and come work a normal day with the chaplain.'

Very tempting!
Yes, it was. And the offers were good-hearted, people really reaching out with much caring. But I couldn't accept because in my opinion non-combatants in the military share in responsibility for the effect of war as much as the one actually pulling the trigger. The military itself points out that for one person to go into combat there must be 11 others in support work — in offices, kitchens, hospitals, etc.

Also there is the fact that, whether one is a nurse or a commander, you are in fact wearing the uniform of the South African Defence Force, which inevitably implies to whomever sees you on the street your practical support of the government and its policies.

Finally, I object to *all* military training. The only way a soldier can be effective is to deny the humanity of his opponent: he is a terrorist, a fascist, a nazi, a communist, a racist — whatever word in a given context that makes him better dead than alive. An object. You cannot afford to think of that person as a husband, father, brother, uncle. You consciously repress any sense of connection, and in de-humanising the other, you lessen your own humanity as well. Military training relies on this process of repression, seeks to obliterate individual identity and to introduce unquestioning obedience without consideration of generally accepted moral values of not killing or desecrating another person.

In that case, why not simply leave the country?
I considered this. In the end I realised that wherever I might go — Britain or Europe or the US — there too I would encounter situations of injustice and violence just as I encounter them in South Africa. So I would not really be avoiding anything. Also, I felt that I should, in a public way, do what was in my power to challenge the whole military service system in our country. In my opinion it would have been useless to attempt that challenge from a distance. By taking this stand right where I was, the challenge would be more difficult to overlook. I wanted to say, in a public way, that I disagree with the way our country functions and, at the same time, to say what I do believe — in forgiveness, in sharing, in just relations between people.

Charles Yeats is now in a military prison for reasons similar to your own. I gather this had something to do with the fact of you and Peter Moll being in prison rather than in exile.
Yes. Charles had gone to Britain. Apparently he read about us in the British press. It touched him and made him decide that if we could go to prison, he could as well.

When were you actually called-up?
16 January, 1980. But, surprisingly, imprisonment was delayed. I went with my little bag with toothbrush, etc. But they told me to go home and that they would let me know when my trial was. So I had an extraordinary walk home again. It was like being reprieved from the dead.

A real Lazarus walk!
It truly was. So I had another six weeks at home to prepare myself and be quiet.

When was the trial?
The afternoon of 25 February. I was found guilty of failing to report without good reason and sentenced to 12 months with six months suspended for three years. From the trial I went directly to military prison.

What was the situation of your imprisonment?
It was a military detention barracks in Pretoria with about 300 offenders — soldiers who had been absent without leave, drunk on duty, guilty of theft, etc. They were being punished for stepping out of line and being treated in such a way that they would never do so again. The life was considerably more rugged than the ordinary military situation.

No Sunday-school picnic.
Most decidedly not. It was far more difficult than I had anticipated. If I had

known beforehand how difficult it was going to be, I probably would have opted for leaving the country. It was God's grace that shielded me from knowing what it would be like until I was actually there. It was a place of systematic humiliation, with the intention to de-humanise, to strip the person of his uniqueness. In a military structure, you cannot afford individuality. You must only have the *unit* — all reacting to orders without questions. The purpose of the prison is to eradicate that part of the person which has resulted in disobedience.

But I know you refused to obey, refused to wear the uniform, refused military drills, as a result of which you spent quite some time in solitary confinement. How long?
In all, 52 days in the first six months. Finally they accepted my refusal to live a military life.

Until that acceptance occurred, what were your confrontations with those in charge like?
The sergeant major might come up and, standing two inches from my face and speaking in a parade ground shout, order me to wear the uniform. And then I would respond, quite gently and simply, 'No, sergeant major, I do not wish to wear this uniform. It is against my principles for the following reasons . . .' I purposely dropped my voice and did not exhibit any anger back towards him.

What was the response?
It took him completely off balance. It was extraordinary to watch the reaction. They are used to grovelling obedience — absolute, unthinking, immediate — as if the officer were God. For someone to disobey, and not to exhibit fear in the disobedience, was quite an experience. Finally they just didn't give me orders anymore, perhaps because it was too embarrassing when I refused.

You say that you didn't exhibit *anger and fear. But surely you* felt *them.*
I often felt anger, especially at what I saw going on around me — the way others were beaten to the ground.

How did you deal with the anger?
I cried frequently. I would get a point where I would just cry — and that would give some physical relief from the tension.

Was crying a rare event in the barracks?
Not at all. It's extraordinary. Soldiers are taught to be tough, but when you get down to it, they're human like the rest of us. So there was crying when it was just too much for someone.

What sort of things were 'too much'?
There was one day, after a relatively relaxed period, when the sergeant major was in such a bad mood that he took it out on the prisoners being drilled. In the afternoon, after hard drilling, they were made to run up and down a hill with wheelbarrows of sand. At supper time one chap was in such a state that,

breaking the rule of silence at meals, he said something — I don't know what. The corporal on duty made the soldiers 'leopard crawl' — crawl on elbows and knees — from the mess hall to the barracks, across gravel, up stone steps, across concrete. I wouldn't myself, of course, but everyone else did, and by the time we were in the barracks everyone's elbows and knees were cut and bleeding, a bloody mess, awful. Straight after supper. They were so humiliated!

How did you respond to the situation?
It happened to be an evening that I had a bible study with the prisoners. So these chaps who came along discussed the event, because that is what we tried to do, to relate the gospels to daily events.

I recall one of the men wondering about the particular corporal who had given the order to leopard crawl. He was married and lived at home. 'I wonder what happens if his wife burns the toast,' he put it. 'Does he order her to leopard crawl around the table?' He was making the connection between what the corporal was doing when he was on shift and when he was at home. When you hate in one context, it pours into the other as well.

How did the bible study groups get going?
It was soon found out that I was a Christian, although I'm not too happy throwing that label around. It's too narrowly defined. You get easily dismissed. But it got known. People would ask why I wasn't wearing the uniform or doing drills, so I would explain my refusal to participate in war because of my belief that life is holy. The Christian rationale would come out quite quickly. Many would come back to talk more intimately — they perhaps would want more of a personal relationship with God. It got to a stage when it became obvious we ought to get together as a group and so we met a couple of evenings a week.

How is prison as an environment for this kind of study?
The bible has to do with living and suffering. The prison situation is so foreign and hostile that you are forced to re-think very basic questions. So it wasn't difficult to have a bible study — in fact an ideal place.

I remember one evening, at the end, when we were about to have a time of prayer and were talking about what to pray about. One of the group suggested, 'Let's pray for the boys on the border fighting the terrorists.' I said, 'Fine, Let's do it. But let's pray as well for the SWAPO army.' That absolutely shocked him. It was the first time he's ever thought of praying for — in his opinion — the enemy. We talked about it quite a lot, and he came to see that if you pray for one person, you should pray for another.

The hardest thing for many of them was to realise that the basic defense of the army in South Africa — that it's there to defend Christianity — doesn't stand up to biblical reflection.

Thomas Merton used to say that the root of war is fear. I suppose this must have come up in discussions of events of the day and the larger military purpose.

It did. Through it I came increasingly to realise that fear is one of the crucial areas that needs to be dealt with by peace and justice workers. For myself the great crossing point came before prison, when I had to consider the possibility of death, that I might die in prison. I could imagine that under some circumstances a person might get beaten to death. Was I prepared to die for what I believed? I realised finally that I was, and this freed me of a tremendous anxiety.

In prison itself, in refusing to obey orders, while no longer worrying about death, there was fear at first about solitary confinement or being put on 'spare diet' — bread and water — as I was at one point.

One of the things that I learned was not to get preoccupied with physical consequences and rather to concentrate on the actual value of what I was doing. Let the consequences take care of themselves.

The *power* of fearlessness is astonishing. I think of those who were giving me orders. They were under a real tyranny and far more the victim of it than I was. When they were yelling their orders at me, I had a vivid image of these tiny creatures assaulting my feet, wanting to demolish me with orders, while I was way above, not on their level at all. They could threaten me with anything at all and not get me, because I wasn't afraid. This was immensely liberating to me. I could be the person I was without fearing them. They had no power over me.

How did you spend your time while in solitary confinement?
Yoga, long periods of prayer, bible study, recalling and reliving events in my life. It helped simply to accept the reality of a small cell and its isolation and then expand my consciousness as far as it would go. You come to realise very clearly that God isn't locked in or out of corrugated iron walls, that Jesus suffered in similar ways and overcame the power of evil confronting him.

Did you not feel anger at being punished in that way?
Quite often rage just tears me apart. Yes, I felt it. The rage most often led to a real crying within me. On a spiritual level, the way I have coped is to talk to God. You realise God is sharing the same rage, the same pain — that God is here with me, seeing whatever I'm seeing, experiencing what I am experiencing. No bolt of lightning, just sharing. And that's helpful, to know God's accompanying me in it, and others as well.

Does the experience of anger build a bridge with others whose anger has led them to violence?
Absolutely. I can really understand why people choose violence. I can understand the frustration, the anger, the helplessness in the face of the *massive*, monolithic structure of apartheid. Many people have tried dialogue and disciplined ways of nonviolent resistance, and been smashed. I can understand choosing violence: to watch a bomb explode, to see something happen. If I weren't a Christian, I don't know where my anger would take me. Yet I know, in the long run, violence doesn't heal.

Do you have any hope for change among white South Africans? You have come a long way yourself . . .
I believe no person is hopeless, worthless, totally bad, totally wrong. There is always an element of goodness in each person and the possibility of change. In detention barracks I was able to build really human relations with other prisoners and with the prison staff, though it took time. I saw profound changes in attitude toward me and toward the issue of conscientious objection. There is always the possibility of change, even among the whites governing the country.

To what extent, in the Christianity of South Africa, is there a potential for real breakthrough against racism?
In the white Afrikaner church of South Africa, there is certainly a genuine desire to please and serve God and to introduce God's kingdom. Many truly believe apartheid is genuinely what God desires, and see themselves in a group with the light, leading the rest of the population into the light through their policies. But their desire to serve God is very strong. If they could just alter their perspective, widen their sense of God, that same commitment and energy would be immensely valuable to us.

Is there already a crisis of conscience underway within white South African Christianity in regard to racism and apartheid?
Definitely. It is now to a point where people in Afrikaans church leadership and in the government realise they can no longer justify theologically the apartheid system. Old theological theses are increasingly seen as indefensible, without a genuine biblical basis.

Are you still intent to return to South Africa?
Yes. God calls us to serve people, and the people I know best are South Africans. So I'm committed to returning. God desires healing and sharing. Therefore I want to work for that in the South African situation.

How free will you be to do that?
I don't know. It is quite possible that when I step off the plane, I will be arrested on the spot. There may have been new call-up papers issued to me while I have been out of the country, or they might arrest me simply because they think it would be dangerous for me to be loose. But, no matter what happens, I feel it's important to be there.

In any event, when I think of other places I might live, none of them seem as open to the creation of a new society as South Africa, and it is certainly a place where I feel a responsibility to do what I can to mobilise nonviolent action for liberation, to do what I can to mobilise the kind of conscience that gives people the awareness and strength to disobey unjust laws.

There are already quite a number in South Africa that say they believe in integration and sharing. Let's *do* that. Let's live together. Let's ride on the train together. Let's share neighbourhoods together. Let us give a specifically nonviolent input into the liberation struggle, and at the same time offer an indication of what the new society will be like.

Are you at all hopeful that the changeover, in a general sense, could be nonviolent?
As things are now, one can hardly imagine it — rather a really bitter civil war. But for those of us committed to nonviolence, whatever may come, we have an important role to play. I don't myself know all the specifics yet. I feel I'm very much on pilgrimage at the moment, learning. But I know when the moment comes to return, the way ahead will make itself clear.

Neil Mitchell (1982 Statement)

Why I am a Universal Pacifist Conscientious Objector

REASONS FOR CONSCIENTIOUS OBJECTION

A. Introduction

I am a Christian, a baptised and confirmed member of the Roman Catholic Church. I take my faith seriously, and after much careful thought, prayer and study over several years, I came to a decision to refuse to undergo military service. I thus declare myself a universal pacifist conscientious objector to military service.

I believe that my decision is in accordance with the spirit of the life and teachings of Jesus Christ. Following Christ, which I am to do, involves being a 'peacemaker' — 'Blessed are the peacemakers; they shall be called sons of God' (Mt 5: 9). Participating in war, training for war or performing violent acts is, I believe, antithetical to the call to be a peacemaker.

B. Violence and killing

1. The Old Testament .

God created the world in a state of 'shalom' (Gen 2) — peace and harmony between God and people and between people and people. People's first act of disobedience alienated them from God and broke this shalom. An instance of this alienation was Cain's killing of Abel (Gen 4: 1-16). God's anger at this violent act is proof to me of the seriousness of killing.

The covenant which God made with Moses at Sinai forbids killing: 'You must not kill' (Ex 20: 13). It also forbids other violent acts (Ex 21: 12-27).

2. Jesus Christ

Jesus, when He instituted the new covenant by His life, death and resurrection, reiterated the command not to kill and made it more radical: 'You have learnt how it was said to our ancestors: "You must not kill", and if anyone does kill he must answer for it before the court. But I say this to you: Anyone who is angry with his brother will answer for it before the court; if a man calls his brother "Fool" he will answer for it before the Sanhedrin; and if a man calls him "Renegade" he will answer for it in hell fire' (Mt 5: 21,22).

The new standard which Jesus sets is higher than the old — we are not even to be angry with or contemptuous of fellow persons.

Jesus went further than just forbidding killing; His whole mission and teaching was in fact life-affirming. He demonstrated to people a loving way of conducting human relationships that would enable them to live peaceably with each other. In all of His actions, Jesus promoted life and wholeness and he sought to remove hostility. He healed the sick, such as the sick man at the pool of Bethzatha (Jn 5: 1-9); he multiplied loaves and fishes to feed the hungry (Jn 6: 1-15). He did not condemn an adulterous woman, but rather encouraged her to sin no more (Jn 8: 3-11). He associated with the outcasts of society — lepers (Lk 17: 11-19), tax collectors (Lk 19: 1-10) and prostitutes (Lk 7: 36-50) — thereby recognising their humanity and that they were as redeemable as others. He cast out demons from people (Mt 17: 14-18). He associated with a Samaritan woman when Jews did not associate with Samaritans (Jn 4: 5-10). He showed his rejection of violence when he admonished Peter for cutting off the high priest's servant's ear, and he healed the man's ear (Lk 22: 47-51). He raised Lazarus from the dead (Jn 11: 43,44). Jesus made possible the reconciliation of all people to God and to God's will. Through His supreme sacrifice on the cross He destroyed the power of death and won salvation and eternal life for all people. He reigns now as the Risen Lord, giving life to all who enter the covenant He has established.

3. The Teaching of the Catholic Church

As a Catholic, I am compelled to adhere to the dictates of my church, which, as I interpret them, support my stand:

> 1. The Council proposes to condemn the savagery of war, and earnestly to exhort Christians to co-operate with all in securing a peace based on justice and charity and in promoting the means necessary to attain it, under the help of Christ, author of peace.
>
> *(Vatican II, Gaudium et Spes, par. 77)*
>
> 2. Let us . . . take stock of our responsibilities and find ways of resolving our controversies in a manner worthy of human beings. Providence urgently demands of us that we free ourselves from the age-old slavery of war. If we refuse to make this effort, there is no knowing where we will be led on the fatal path we have taken.
>
> *(Vatican II, Gaudium et Spes, par. 81)*
>
> 3. It is your clear duty to spare no effort in order to work for the moment when all war will be completely outlawed by international agreement.
>
> *(Vatican II, Gaudium et Spes, par. 82)*
>
> 4. Nothing is lost by peace; everything may be lost by war.
>
> *(Pope Pius XII, Radio Message, 24 August 1939)*
>
> 5. Is there anyone who does not ardently yearn to see dangers of war banished, to see peace preserved and daily more firmly established?
>
> *(Pope John XXIII, Pacem in Terris, par. 115)*
>
> 6. Never again must one land make war against another. No more War! Not ever again. Peace! Peace must guide the destinies of peoples and of human beings.
>
> *(Pope Paul VI)*
>
> 7. Violence is a lie, for it goes against the truth of our faith, the truth of our humanity . . . do not believe in violence. It is not the Christian way. It is not

the way of the Catholic Church. Believe in peace and forgiveness and love; for they are of Christ.
Give yourselves to the service of life, not to the work of death . . . true courage lies in working for peace.

(Pope John Paul II, Drogheda, Ireland)

Throughout these pronouncements, the Catholic Church makes clear its abhorrence of war and violence. I wish to align myself with the spirit of these pronouncements.

C. Nonviolent ways of dealing with conflict, based on Jesus' teaching

I believe that war and preparation for war deny Jesus' teaching on dealing with conflict. Jesus teaches that we must not retaliate: 'You have learnt how it was said: Eye for eye and tooth for tooth. But I say this to you: Offer the wicked man no resistance. On the contrary, if anyone hits you on the right cheek, offer him the other as well' (Mt 5: 38-39).

He says further: 'You have learnt how it was said: You must love your neighbour and hate your enemy. But I say this to you: love your enemies and pray for those who persecute you; in this way you will be sons of your Father in heaven' (Mt 5: 43-45). Christians are told: 'Never repay evil with evil but let everyone see that you are interested only in the highest ideals. Do all you can to live at peace with everyone. Never try to get revenge . . . Resist evil and conquer it with good' (Rom 12: 17-19,21); and they are warned: 'Those who live by the sword will die by the sword' (Mat 26: 52).

In the spirit of Jesus' teaching, I believe that conflict must be resolved without resort to violence, but rather in a manner that is worthy of human beings. Primarily, dialogue and negotiation must be employed, and conflict situations must be entrusted to divine providence (Lk 12: 22-31; Mat 26: 53). In the event of an enemy invasion, nonviolent means, such as marches, vigils, demonstrations, sit-ins, strikes, boycotts, non-payment of taxes, non-co-operation (a government cannot rule without the consent of the people), civil disobedience and physical interpositioning, can be used to make a moral appeal to the heart and conscience of the enemy, in the hope of winning him over to a position of truth. The whole defence system of a country could be organised to employ such nonviolent means, rather than arms.

A fraction of what is normally spent on equipping and maintaining an army would have to be spent on organising and training for, and doing research into, such a nonviolent defence system. Greater financial resources could then be allocated to such needs as housing, education, health and agriculture. Nonviolent means of defence lend a moral dignity to those who use them, and, since they incorporate the recognition that there is something in people which is higher than the brute nature in them, these means are worthy of human beings.

D. How all of this affects my response to my call-up instructions

1. Obedience to my call-up instructions is incompatible with the nature of my relationship with God — violence is sinful.

To obey my call-up instructions and go to the army would, for me, constitute

91

a betrayal of my covenant relationship with God which I have entered through my baptism. I feel a responsibility to honour this relationship since it was bought with the price of Christ's shed blood. I cannot go against it in good conscience. By the transforming power of the Holy Spirit, this relationship changes me into a new being, called to be perfect: 'You must be perfect just as your heavenly Father is perfect' (Mt 5: 48). I must follow Christ's example and avoid sin — 'You have stripped off your old behaviour with your old-self, and you have put on a new self which will progress towards true knowledge the more it is renewed in the image of its creator' (Col 3: 9). It is clear to me through Christ's teaching and example that violence and killing are sinful. I therefore cannot in good conscience participate in war (the most overt form of violence) or training for war, or be part of an institution whose purpose is to wage war. War is antithetical to Christ's way of healing and loving.

2. Dehumanisation of the enemy
Furthermore, army training would condition me into dehumanising the enemy into a thing to be hated. I could not in good conscience go along with such a process, since it denies the enemy's humanity and his bearing of the image and likeness of God. I am commanded by Christ to love all people, including enemies.

3. The 'service of life'
I wish, in the words of Pope John Paul II, to give myself to the 'service of life,' not to the 'work of death'. I wish, in my life, to promote peace and justice, which the world in general, and South Africa in particular, sorely need. I cannot see that participating in army training would aid me in my endeavour to be a peacemaker.

4. Non-military national service
I believe that I have a duty and a responsibility to contribute to the well-being and prosperity of my country. I am thus willing to do a non-military form of National Service. For this reason, too, I chose not to leave South Africa in order to avoid having to go to the army. I am a fully qualified high school teacher; I could use these qualifications and skills in an alternative, non-military form of national service.

E. Pacifism and world conditions today

1. Does pacifism have any relevance?
I am aware that many regard pacifism as naive, unrealistic and inappropriate for the complexity of today's world, which encompasses enormous stockpiling of arms (including nuclear armaments), polarisation between the East and the West, cold war antagonism, open warfare, active liberation and guerrilla movements advocating armed conflict, discrimination, injustice, and oppression. Yet I feel that it is these very trends which validate the pacifist position. As *Gaudium et Spes* warns, unless governments find ways of solving conflict that do not include resort to warfare, mankind, and the earth along with him, is headed for destruction. War must be outlawed and the escalating slide towards this destruction averted.

2. Christians and pacifism

Universal Christian pacifism, to which I hold, is an absolute ethical principle, drawn from the teachings of Jesus Christ (especially the Sermon on the Mount). The early Christians had a tradition of non-participation in war — the theologian Tertullian, for example, counselled Christians not to go to war. Through the centuries the church, taking cognisance of people's inclination towards self-defence, developed a 'just war' theory, which permitted Christians to wage war if certain conditions were met. Even the 'just war' theory becomes obsolete since its condition that innocents and non-combatants must not be harmed during warfare, with the use of modern weapons, is no longer met. National armies, uniforms, military music and parades, medals, badges, war toys, the belief that it is 'glorious' to die in 'active service' in the defence of one's country, the belief that going to the army 'makes a man of you' — all these have institutionalised and legitimised violence. Society has been conditioned into regarding war as normal and acceptable.

Christians have an appalling record when it comes to warfare. Horrendous situations have arisen where Catholics have fought against each other on opposite sides of a border, and where different Catholic bishops, aligned to different sides, have blessed the weapons of nations warring against each other. This hardly bears testimony to the love of Christ and to the unity of believers. I believe Christians must take seriously the teachings of their Lord, apply them, and return with an urgency to their roots as a peaceful people who say *no* to war. It is not Christian pacifism which has failed; it is Christians who have failed to apply the principles of pacifism.

F. Conclusion

I am aware that I am contravening a section of the Defence Act of South Africa, and I am aware of the legal consequences of such a contravention. Nevertheless, I believe that I have informed my conscience in this matter, and my conscience urges me to take this stand. To go against my conscience is sin. 'Obedience to God comes before obedience to men' (Acts 5: 29).

Billy Paddock (Interview, August 1982)

A pacifist stance is a common form of conscientious objection generally accepted by the authorities in most Western countries. How is your position different?

I believe a universal pacifist stance is impossible because we are all involved in various forms of violence in many different aspects of our lives. Violence is not just a physical encounter between two or more people. It is built into structures. It concerns the way we deal with our environment. The mere fact of paying taxes is a form of supporting violence because they go to the police, the army, and to the government in South Africa who have created and who continue to maintain a law system built on institutional violence.

My attitude to violence is that I abhor violence, but I accept that people come into conflict situations which cause violence. Within South Africa at this point I believe violent revolution is inevitable, and, while I personally at this stage cannot take up arms, I nevertheless support the overall goal of freedom that the liberation movements are striving for, and I respect the choice of those who have had to take the agonising choice of taking up arms.

For myself, because the whole system is unjust and oppressive, I refuse to do national service which is there to protect and uphold the status quo.

So you cannot accept a universal pacifist position and you also cannot in conscience serve in the South African Defence Force?
Correct. I cannot serve in the SADF because then I would be taking sides with the oppressors, and Christ calls us to take the side of the poor and the oppressed. I also believe that because the undeclared war that South Africa has been waging for the past few years against SWAPO of Namibia and the ANC of South Africa is unjustified, I cannot take up arms against them. As a Christian therefore it is not permissible for me to join the army.

What do you think though of South Africa's claim that their forces are merely fighting the extension of communism in southern Africa and that the ANC and SWAPO are committing terrorism?
That is Government propaganda. Churchill wasn't labelled a communist in World War II when he fought alongside of and received help from the Soviet Union. ANC and SWAPO were initially refused help from Western nations, and only then did they turn to the Eastern bloc countries for help. It is under the guise of this communist bogey that South Africa is destabilising the bordering southern African countries of Mozambique, Angola and Zimbabwe, and forcing them to become economically dependent on South Africa.

What sort of support have you received for your stand from your family and your church?
I have received very little support from either my family or the official church. The support from the church has mainly been that they would pray for me, and in doing so they are accepting that it is up to the individual's conscience whether to fight or not fight in the SADF. But for the true church, which is the believing and acting people of God, I have received a great deal of moral and material support.

It would seem though to the casual observer to be a lot easier for you to simply leave the country. Why don't you leave?
I love South Africa. I love its people. I believe I can contribute more to South Africa from within the country than from outside. I believe the struggle for liberation must be waged though from both fronts — from within and from outside the country. I respect those who choose to go into exile to carry on the struggle there. I feel that my best contribution can come from within, and I do not believe the solution for me is to leave the country.

How are you feeling with the prospect of gaol looming larger every day?
Nervous, apprehensive, quite afraid.

But you still plan to go through with it?
Yes, I will definitely go through with it. I have no other option. The fact that it is inevitable that I will be found guilty is an example of the kind of laws which govern this country, which make no provision for a person's conscience. The irony of it is that they ask you to swear the oath and accept God's word as binding on your conscience, and then punish someone for doing just that. They acknowledge the supremacy of God both in the Constitution of the country and the court of law, and yet my whole court case is about my right to observe the supremacy of God and God's law.

But, believe me, I am at peace with myself and the position I have taken.

Why I say No to collaboration with the SADF (1982 Statement)

My attitude to violence
In a society where life expectancy is twice as high in the upper as in the lower classes, violence is exercised even if there are no concrete instances that one can point to of direct attack. As Christians, can we discuss this from a neutral standpoint, above or outside a situation of violence? We are actively involved in a system which is violent to the degree that it denies, through its laws and social structure, to the majority of the population a large amount of its actualisation. This could be avoided if the system were different. We are all involved as oppressors or oppressed by paying taxes, acting as marriage officers and doing military service. Who stands behind the policeman who fires into the crowd?

Violence can have structural forms built into the apparently peaceful operations of society as well as overt physical expressions. The failure to provide educational opportunities, or the manipulation of sources of information, can do violence to those affected.

What options do I, as a Christian, have within this society in which I live? I recognise that we are all already involved as participants in violence. For many Christians who find themselves in acute situations of social injustice nonviolence would mean a total withdrawal from the struggle in South Africa. A relatively just order must be established before violence can cease. I believe it is hypocrisy when Christians in positions of privilege endorse violence (in all its masks) on behalf of a biased law and order but invoke moral denunications against violence that threatens the unjust order.

I know that I would rather be shot a hundred times than shoot another person. I hate violence. Yet I am part of it. I accept the urgent necessity for a radical change of structures and recall that J.F. Kennedy once said 'Those who make peaceful revolutions impossible will make violent revolution inevitable'.

I see the South African regime's intransigence and refusal to allow a peaceful revolution to take place and I accept the fact that those who take up arms as a last resort see the necessity of violent resistance and I respect their agonising choice and risk. I cannot preach patient endurance of a suffering I don't have to bear directly and I cannot withhold my support from those who have decided on this road.

How do I humanise the means of conflict?

I know that this demands a radical stand. It demands a passion of compassion and 'violent non-violence' (Helder Camara). It demands identification with the poor and the oppressed and their cause. It demands dissociation from a system of structural violence wherever possible. It demands a prophetic denunciation of a repressive system in *deeds and words*. It demands revolutionary gestures of protest and hope (like Jesus' cleansing of the Temple). It demands to adopt the life-style of the future Kingdom. It demands suffering, it might demand persecution or imprisonment.

The early Christian church believed in the imminent coming of God's kingdom and held on to the belief that soon judgment would come and that justice will be done. They therefore took up a pacifist stance. As time progressed and the Kingdom 'in all its glory' did not come the church was faced with a dilemma with regard to war. St Augustine drew up a series of criteria for war which later became the just war theory. All the mainstream churches have held to this theory/doctrine up to the present day. It is one of the official articles of the Anglican Church of which I am a member. I am obliged therefore to translate or interpret the doctrines of this church in my life. I do not purely accept the just war theory for myself because it is one of the 39 articles. I believe that it still has validity today.

The just war doctrine has validity only when it is applied within the context of a socio-economic and political analysis which then gives the criteria meaning. In the absence of such an analysis it is merely a set of unconnected phrases.

I cannot enter the SADF because of the role it plays in defending the structural violence of the South African system. I am then confronted with two options: to leave the country or to object. I did not want to leave the country as I believe I have a role to play in liberating the peoples of this country from oppression and exploitation. I believe I can do this best by remaining in the country and committing myself to this struggle and having an obligation to resistance. I chose to object because once I have sided with the oppressed and exploited it becomes virtually impossible to speak of strategic involvement in the military because I would then be siding with the oppressor.

I do not believe there is such a status as a non-combatant in the South African situation. Magnus Malan has stated that it takes six to seven 'non-combatants' to keep one combatant in the field. I believe objection is a very valid option today because whites need to take sides and need to be seen to be taking sides. I believe this is one clear way of joining the struggle for a democratic South Africa.

There are eight criteria by reference to which a war might be declared 'just'.

    1. The war must be *declared by a legitimate authority;* it must not be the expression of a private grudge or waged out of revenge.

    2. The war must be *waged for a just cause;* it must be waged in defense

of a country against attack or else to right a wrong one state has inflicted on another.

3. The war must be *carried out with a right or good intention;* it must be motivated by the good of justice for the purpose of peace.
4. The war must have *a reasonable chance of success;* unless there is a good chance that the objective for waging war can be achieved, it is immoral to incur the damage and destruction that will result.
5. The war must be undertaken *only as a last resort;* it can not be just as long as there is *any* chance of resolving the conflict by discussion, negotiation, sanctions or other means short of military action.
6. The war must be waged on the basis of the *principle of proportion;* the good to be accomplished must outweigh the evil that will be exercised in bringing about the good.
7. The war must be carried out *with just means;* there must be a limited use of force and the immunity of non-combatants must be respected.
8. After the war a situation of *a just peace must prevail;* that peace and justice will follow rather than tyranny.

. . . Let us apply the criteria of the just war doctrine to the war the SADF is presently waging in South Africa and Namibia.

1. The war must be declared by a legitimate authority

The war has never been declared. The decision to enter into the war situation was not taken by the legislative body (parliament), as it should have, but rather was taken by the executive body (cabinet). With respect to the war being conducted in Namibia the war was not only not declared but South Africa has no legitimate authority in that country and the SADF is in fact an illegal occupying force in another country.

. . . In South Africa it can also be argued that the government is not the legitimate authority. According to Thomas Aquinas a legitimate authority is that government constituted for the common good to administer and distribute justice. Aquinas states that when a government stops doing this it loses its legitimacy. This is based on natural law.

The preamble to the South African Constitution recognises the supremacy of God and the responsibility of the administrators to administer for the good of all. This slots into Aquinas' framework. However with the plethora of unjust and exploitative laws and the method of implementing these the South African government has stopped administering for the common good and has never fully distributed justice. Therefore it has lost its legitimacy.

In 1960 the government held a referendum which led to the establishment of the Republic. Africans, who constituted approximately 70% of the population of South Africa were not entitled to vote, and were not even consulted about the proposed constitutional change. Clearly then, in terms of democracy (which the government claims exists in South Africa), this government is not legitimate. And even if it was legitimately constituted as an oligarchy it has no authority and the regime is not a legitimate authority but rather a tyranny. This was shown very clearly on 21 March 1960 when the government violently repressed a peaceful demonstration and killed 69 people and wounded many others. It had happened many times before, and since, clearly demonstrating that the government has no authority among the majority of the country's citizens.

2. The war must be waged for a just cause

The South African government states that there is a 'total onslaught' against the state from the 'communists of Moscow'. The South African government propaganda together with the 'official opposition', the PFP, persist in their 'anti-communist' rhetoric. The persistance with this stance represents either a complete misunderstanding of South African history or a deliberate attempt at mystifying the issues in this country.

The growth of the SADF can be more or less traced back to 1961, with two events sparking off that growth. On 31 May the White Republic was established, marking the final consolidation of National Party vote. And just six months later the first act of sabotage was committed by Umkhonto we Sizwe. The African National Congress was formed in 1912 and over the following 49 years every peaceful means of protest against the racist South African state and against the institutions of oppression and exploitation, had been attempted. For many the last straw was the Sharpeville demonstration of March 1960, in which 69 unarmed people were massacred by the police. The subsequent banning of the ANC and PAC convinced many that further peaceful protest was futile and constitutional means, which the propaganda claims is the way for change, was not and is not open to blacks.

It is within this context that the first ANC guerrillas left for training, with the aim of mounting a campaign of limited sabotage against government installations throughout the country to try to discourage foreign capital and thereby hoping to get the white electorate to reconsider their position. The emphasis was on installations not individuals. The ANC sought aid from the Western countries first and only when this was not forthcoming did they turn to the Eastern bloc. The supply of aid from 'communist' countries does not necessarily make the liberation movements communist or 'puppets of Moscow'. When the allied forces in World War II fought alongside communist Russia, Churchill was not labelled a 'communist' nor did he or the allied forces become 'communists' as a result of working together on the same side.

The SADF is engaged in a war against blacks who have fled this country's oppressive and exploitative system, many of them school pupils who fled after clashes with the police in 1976 and 1977. Both the Steyn Commission and the Rabie Commission attest to this fact. Thus the war is a civil war and not a war of defence against some external faceless oppressor.

South Africa's generals often talk of a 'total onslaught' on South Africa. There is a total onslaught — not by a faceless Russian bear — but by the forces of democracy in South Africa in the schools, in the universities, in the factories and in the communities.

3. The war must be carried out with a right or good intention

South African society has been regarded as unjust and oppressive for a long time now. A lot of the critics have held to the myth that racial segregation in South Africa began with the coming to power of the National Party in 1948. In fact racial exploitation has been a feature of South African society ever since the first whites settled here. Largely through superior military might, the white settlers were able to force the indigenous people off their land and into relations of servitude as slaves or indentured labourers or as labour tenants who were forced to pay rent in cash, kind or labour services to the settlers.

Thus from early on racial discrimination was clearly bound up with the exploitation of labour. This relationship was reinforced with the discovery of diamonds in 1867, and gold in 1886. Conditions of production in the mining industry required a plentiful supply of cheap labour. This was provided by the further disintegration of African agriculture through the imposition of taxes and the expropriation of land. Various laws were passed culminating in the 1913 Land Act, which allocated 13% of the land to the entire African population. African peasants were no longer able to support themselves out of their own production and were thus forced to go and work on the mines and farms. Pass laws were used to ensure that the required number went to the various areas of employment. The employers benefited directly from this emerging migrant labour system because of the low wages they could pay.

In addition, at Union in 1910, blacks — except for a tiny minority in the Cape — were denied the franchise. The vote became the key factor for white workers. Also highly exploited by the low-paying industrialists, the white workers used their vote to push for change and reserve for themselves the higher-paid jobs. Largely through the pressure of white workers (e.g. the 1922 Mine Workers' Strike) the Pact government came to power in 1924. It immediately pushed through legislation entrenching the colour bar and job reservation, and creating areas of state employment (e.g. Escom and Iscor) for white workers. This grouping of white workers and civil servants became — and remain — dependent on racial discrimination to maintain their positions.

But the demands of the increasingly sophisticated urban blacks were a constant threat to the system. The white response was to tighten political control and repression. The mechanisms of control were established on their present basis by the National Party governments of the 1950s.

The boom conditions of the 1960s gave way to the worst recession South Africa had ever experienced and once again the growing crisis confronting the state became manifest. The crisis was an ensemble of simultaneous and mutually determining economic, political and ideological crises. Simultaneously the state faced a crisis within itself with the information debacle and the split in the ruling party.

It is in this context that certain sectors of big business, of the military and of the more 'verligte' wing of the government began devising strategies to cope with the crisis. In responding to these dynamics these groups found that their new interests were converging: a total strategy was being formed. The overriding concern was the need to secure immediate domestic stability. The military was calling for more 'defensible policies' and big business was calling for reforms. The emergence of total strategy was not 'inevitable' in any sense but like apartheid, was one option open to the state in maintaining the status quo.

In essence, the strategy involved a concerted attempt to encourage and develop an upper stratum of blacks and create a so-called 'middle class'. This group would help meet the skilled labour shortages, enlarge the consumer market and act as a buffer group against the aspirations and initiatives of the majority of oppressed and exploited workers and rural subsistence dwellers. They would play this role because they would be offered a sufficient enough stake in the system to be prepared to defend it. Clearly, for this strategy to even begin to succeed it was necessary that apartheid be reformed — in P.W. Botha's words, 'We must adapt, or we will die!' So from 1977 onwards a series of restructuring initiatives began to be implemented.

As P.W. Botha has said with regard to the restructuring: the goal is 'to achieve the national aims within the framework of the specific policies' (Defence White Paper 1977:5) which in essence is the same as his 'adapt or die' statement, i.e. adapting apartheid not dismantling it. Essentially we have a more sophisticated and better looking form of oppression and exploitation. We continue to have the Nyangas, the Limehills, the Dimbazas, the Kwa Pitelas, the totally preventable cholera and malnutrition, detention without trial and deaths in detention, etc.

This is the policy General Magnus Malan has stated that the SADF supports, when in 1979 he said 'The Defence Force supports government policy . . . This policy is the same as that laid down by Dr H.F. Verwoerd, namely multinationalism and self-determination of nations'.

4. The war must have a reasonable chance of success

The war has been described by the military leades as being '80% socio-economic and only 20% military. If we lose the socio-economic struggle then we need not even bother to fight the military one' (Gen G.J.J. Boshoff in PRP Journal *Progress* June 1976).

Gen Malan put it rather differently: 'Bullets kill bodies, not beliefs. I would like to remind you that the Portuguese did not lose the military battle in Angola and Mozambique (sic), but they lost the faith and trust of the inhabitants of these countries' (*Daily News* 13.6.1979).

In line with this, the SADF has embarked on a campaign to win the 'hearts and minds' of the oppressed people through their Civic Action Programme (CAP) . . . However, the hostility to the SADF in Northern Namibia, which comprises approximately half of the population, suggests that this strategy is not successful. In the SACBC's report on Namibia we can see why it is failing:

> Reports of what occurs in the operational area indicate that it is commonly accepted that in searching out SWAPO guerrillas the Security Forces stop at nothing to force information out of people. They break into homes, beat up residents, shoot people, steal and kill cattle and often pillage stores and tea rooms. When the tracks of SWAPO guerrillas are discovered by the security forces the local people are in danger. Harsh measures are intensified. People are blindfolded, taken from their houses and left beaten up and even dead by the roadside. Women are often raped (p.20).

Colonel Martins told journalists recently, 'In Ovamboland (where almost half of Namibians live) I'm not sure the hearts and minds strategy does much good because of large numbers of SWAPO there' (*Financial Times* 12.2.1981). This was confirmed by a group of *Sunday Times* journalists after a recent tour: 'While the army is winning the military conflict in the border war it appears that in Kavango it does not seem to be succeeding in winning the hearts and minds of the people' (*Sunday Times* 7.3.82). And, as Malan, Boshoff and others have said, if we lose the battle for the hearts and minds of the people, we need not even bother to fight the military battle. Maj. Gen. Jannie Geldenhuys, when he was commander in Namibia, made it known that the SADF could not win the war.

This apart, if we focus on the broader political spectrum we can see that central to all the struggles of the oppressed has been their demand for real political power; in other words, full representation at all levels of government on a one-person, one-vote basis. This has been expressed in the resistance to the state's attempts to impose dummy institutions on the people (e.g. the anti-SAIC and anti-Ciskei campaigns), in the increasingly frequent references to the Freedom Charter, or simply through the demand for the recognition of democratic and representative organisations.

In all these struggles the same call has been heard: 'Until you meet our minimum demand for genuine political power, we will reject your reformist moves and continue our struggle'.

The President's Council and the new constitutional proposals, which have been hailed as a 'step in the right direction', have failed entirely to convince the oppressed people that this is a move toward genuine power sharing. In the past few months we have witnessed many of the organisations of the oppressed people condemning the President's Council proposal. In condemning the proposals they have stressed the Freedom Charter as the basis for any real power sharing. The PC proposals are seen to exclude the African people, who constitute 70% of the population, from all levels of meaningful government. John Kane Berman has also clearly demonstrated that there is no intention now or even in the long-term future to include Africans. The proposals retain ethnicity as the basis of restructuring. They retain, too, key institutions of apartheid such as the Group Areas Act. They insert a form of dictatorial rule, reinforcing the trend towards greater centralisation of power. And they ignore entirely the central issues concerning distribution of land and wealth, and the provision of services. These are the minimum issues that blacks demand and until genuine moves are made in this direction the oppressed will not be won over.

5. *The war must be undertaken only as a last resort*
In Namibia, South Africa has shown its reluctance to negotiate a settlement. In South Africa the government has also shown that it will not negotiate with the true leaders of the majority of the people of this country. Rather it bans and imprisons these leaders. Earlier I demonstrated that South Africa tries to set up dummy bodies which are consistently being rejected by the majority. The South African government ignored blacks' protest at the forming of the Republic which was unwanted and excluded them. The South African government has repeatedly ignored and refused first the All-in-Africa

conferences' call for a National Convention and subsequently other groups who have called for a national convention. I have also demonstrated earlier that the South African government is intent on carrying out the policy of apartheid and the mass rejection of this and the new constitutional proposals by the majority of the people has been ignored. The South African regime is not interested in negotiation with blacks in South Africa and prefers repression, with violence to put down any opposition.

6. The war must adhere to the principle of proportionality
In the first instance if there is no reasonable chance of success in winning the war, and I have shown that this is so in the present situation, then no amount of force or violence, loss of life, destruction to land, people and the economy is justified.

In the present situation with the SADF's continual insurgency raids into Angola, Zimbabwe and Mozambique and the deliberate destabilisation of these countries, the bombing of industry there and the 'scorch earth' tactics employed totally denies this principle.

7. The war must be conducted with just means
There have been numerous reports in the newspapers of atrocities committed by the SADF personnel. The reports in newspapers as well as in the SACBC, SACC, BCC tell of killing prisoners of war, torture of local population, detentions and killing for information and raping of women. We have read reports that the SADF 'hot raids' and operations in Angola and Mozambique have indiscriminately killed hundreds of civilians. Reports show that SADF operations no longer discriminate between SWAPO and the People's Army of Angola and have attacked and killed many Angolans where there were no SWAPO personnel in the area. The Cassinga massacre of women and children has received widescale reporting with evidence beyond doubt that it was the SADF. Torture is used systematically by the police and the army, and villagers have been massacred by the SADF on suspicion of supporting guerrillas. See South African Pressclips — *The SADF and Conscientious Objection* (July 1982), SACBC's *Report on Namibia* (June 1982); BCC & CIIR, *Torture — a cancer in our society* by H. Hunke and J. Ellis (1978).

8. The war must result in a just peace
Pope Paul VI stated, 'If you want peace work for justice.' The intention of the war the SADF is waging is for the defence of apartheid. The CPSA and the Roman Catholic Church have stated that apartheid is indefensible because it is unjust and exploitative. Even if the present regime did win the war (which is highly improbable) there would not be a just peace because apartheid and exploitation would prevail. There would be continued white domination, injustice, oppression, detentions without trial, deaths in detention, gross unemployment and removals.

Appendix C

Some statements on Conscientious Objection by Church Authorities outside South Africa

The 1982 British Methodist Conference

The following resolution was accepted by the Conference.

The London District N/W Synod suggests to Conference to

> 1. Declare its support for the sister church in South Africa on its stand on conscientious objection status for those called to fight for an unjust South African government.
> 2. To declare its support for the right to conscientious objection in South Africa.
> 3. To urge the British Government to continue granting asylum to South African war resisters in terms of the United Nations Resolution 33/165 which urges member states to grant asylum to bona fide South African war resisters.

The resolution went to Conference with the following recommendation:

> The Memorials Committee agrees that the refusal of the South African government to respect the objections of its citizens to military service in what they conscientiously believe to be an unjust cause is indeed deplorable. It therefore invites the Conference to express its support for the South African Conference in criticising the South African government's position and to urge the British government to continue granting asylum to bona fide South African conscientious objectors.

UNITED STATES CATHOLIC CONFERENCE

Military Conscription

Testimony submitted to the House Armed Services Committee, March 1971 (extracts)

In their pastoral of November 1968 the American Bishops stated:

> If war is ever to be outlawed, and replaced by more humane and enlightened

institutions rooted in the notion of universal common good, *it will be because the citizens of this and other nations have rejected the tenets of exaggerated nationalism and insisted on principles of non-violent political and civic action* in both the domestic and international spheres. ('Human Life in Our Day', Section: 'The Role of Conscience', emphasis added).

The Second Vatican Council called for an 'entirely new attitude toward war' (*Church in the Modern World*, n.80). This implies that old concepts of armaments and a balance of power are no longer adequate for world peace and security. New means must be sought to insure the common good of the international community.

The ancient but perennial formula reads: Build up a powerful military defense appropriate to the times, and the bigger and better the military hardware, the greater will be the nation's security. However, the lamentable fact is that in the past one hundred years more than 150 million men, women and children have been killed in wars. The terrible madness about this is that multitudes continue to accept this premise, for the hope of achieving peace by merely maintaining the balance of massive, destructive power is a tempting delusion (Cf. *Ibid.*, n.81).

The primary and crucial task, then, is to define the nation's authentic needs, that is, the limits of its national interests. Americans must confront and resolve the question of how to respond to other national systems — political and economic — which differ from ours. When the spirit of nationalism among our government's leadership and the general public becomes so excessive as to induce us to believe that our nation, our system, our people are superior to other nations, we are working against peace and the energies of war are coming alive in the nation. (Cf. *Ibid.*, n.82.) Can we recognise a laudable pluralism among national systems? If we cannot, then the old notions about securing peace will persist, and we will continue to rely on such devices as sophisticated weapons and large mobilised, combat forces.

As a nation, we must commit ourselves, with firm determination, to respect other men and peoples and their dignity. To do otherwise is to place ourselves in a position of self-righteous superiority and to perceive our neighbours' intentions as immoral, ours as moral. The neighbour is thought to be eager to attack and conquer, while we are the peacemakers.

When our nation fears that its national interests are being threatened and war is imminent, we contend that we must seriously examine our consciences to determine to what extent we are being motivated by fear of the loss of economic advantage; what degree of nationalistic pretentions are involved; has a desire for national prestige and political domination crept into our action; has a spirit of militarism become dominant? (Cf. *Ibid.*, n.85.)

In this post-Hiroshima era, with the frightful prospect of war threatening to devastate the planet, men are forced to search for new insights. It is in this spirit — searching for new understandings about war and respecting the judgment of history — that we address the question of military service in the United States.

Conscientious objection and selective conscientious objection — the law should prohibit the drafting of conscientious objectors and selective conscientious objectors.

The draft law as it is presently written makes no provision for selective conscientious objectors, i.e., objectors to particular wars. This is a matter of concern to the Catholic Church since a growing number of religious objectors are Catholics and many of them are selective objectors. This is also a matter of concern to other denominations.

Both the conscientious objector and the selective objector are representative of a twofold development in Catholic teaching regarding war and conscience. The conscientious objector is one who believes that the Gospel imperatives of love and brotherhood exclude the use of organised violence in international affairs. The selective conscientious objector, on the other hand, is one who determines, through the use of moral reasoning, that to fight in a particular war or to serve in a particular branch of the service (for example, in nuclear forces) would be morally wrong.

Selective conscientious objection is rooted in a tradition which is associated with the evolution of the just war doctrine or theory developed by St. Ambrose in the fourth century and later amplified by St. Augustine, St. Thomas Aquinas and other prominent theologians. According to this doctrine, a war is considered just only if it is declared as a last resort and by lawful authority, uses means which are not intrinsically immoral, and follows the principle of proportionality, that is, the good to be achieved by the war must outweigh the evils caused by the conflict.

While the Church does not officially declare some wars just and other wars unjust, the individual Catholic is obliged to follow his conscience. If that conscience impels him not to participate in a particular war, then he sins gravely by taking part in it. The Catholic who follows the just war theory traditionally taught by the Church and objects to a particular war has a basis for his claim: his religious training and belief.

The section of the Selective Service Act which requires that the registrant be conscientiously opposed to participation in war 'in any form' is too restrictive and discriminatory.

In the pastoral letter cited previously, the Catholic bishops recommended:

> . . . a modification of the Selective Service Act making it possible, although not easy, for so-called selective conscientious objectors to refuse — without fear of imprisonment or loss of citizenship — to serve in wars which they consider unjust or in branches of service (e.g., the strategic nuclear forces) which would subject them to the performance of actions contrary to deeply held moral convictions about indiscriminate killing. Some other form of service to the human community should be required of those so exempted. (*Ibid.*, Section: 'The Role of Conscience')

The selective conscientious objector should be given the same provision under the law as the conscientious objector, providing his objection is well-founded and constitutes a sincerely held moral conviction. He should be allowed to state his case before a competent board of judges. By their own admission, some local boards or individual board members do not feel qualified to make judgments about these questions which are often philosophical or religious in nature. Problems in this area could be partially solved if the question of conscientious objection were handled at a higher level than that of the local board, by a special, regional panel appointed specifically for that purpose.

Alternative service programme — We would urge that Congress review the regulations regarding alternative service and investigate the practices of local boards in assigning civilian work. It has been our experience that the administration of the law has not been uniform in this regard. Some local boards correctly interpret the law and allow the registrant to choose from a broad spectrum of work assignments which contribute to 'national health, safety or interest'. There are usually few problems in placing registrants in civilian work which truly benefits the community and utilises the talents of the registrant for truly productive work.

Other local boards, however, appear to operate from the premise that the registrant should be put in a job which tests his sincerity, and therefore, force the registrant to forego a number of job opportunities in order to place him in work which will be disruptive, disagreeable and unpleasant. This style of operation has been encouraged in part by some communications from the National Headquarters of the Selective Service, such as Local Board Memoranda 64 and 98.

If alternative service becomes a form of punishment or a test of sincerity, it can be counterproductive in the long run, negatively affecting the young person's attitude toward service to the human community. It is assumed that the registrant is sincere if his claim is accepted and he is granted an exemption.

The Selective Service System should relax the stringent regulations regarding civilian work in LBM 64 and LBM 98 and provide for a more uniform administration of the programme through the local boards. If that were done, Catholic health and welfare agencies would be able to co-operate more easily with Selective Service in providing jobs for conscientious objectors on alternative service.

Declaration on Conscientious Objection and Selective Conscientious Objection

21 October 1971

For many of our Catholic people, especially the young, the question of participation in military service has become a serious moral problem. They properly look to their spiritual leaders for guidance in this area of moral decision and for support when they judge their sentiments to be in keeping with Catholic Christian tradition. For this reason, we wish to express ourselves on the following principles.

The traditional teaching of the Church regarding the importance of individual conscience is crucial in this issue of conscientious objection and selective conscientious objection. The obligation to seek the truth in order to form right and true judgments of conscience and the obligation to follow conscience was put in positive terms by Pope Paul VI and the Fathers at the Second Vatican Council:

Further light is shed on the subject if one considers that the highest norm of human life is the divine law — eternal, objective, and universal — whereby God orders, directs, and governs the entire universe and all the ways of the human community, by a plan conceived in wisdom and love. Man has been made by God to participate in this law, with the result that, under the gentle disposition of divine Providence, he can come to perceive ever increasingly the unchanging truth. Hence every man has the duty, and therefore the right, to seek the truth in matters religious, in order that he may with prudence form for himself right and true judgments of conscience, with the use of all suitable means.

Truth, however, is to be sought after in a manner proper to the dignity of the human person and his social nature. The inquiry is to be free, carried on with the aid of teaching or instruction, communication, and dialogue. In the course of these, men explain to one another the truth they have discovered, or think they have discovered, in order thus to assist one another in the quest for truth. Moreover, as the truth is discovered, it is by a personal assent that men are to adhere to it.

On his part, man perceives and acknowledges the imperatives of the divine law through the mediation of conscience. In all his activity a man is bound to follow his conscience faithfully, in order that he may come to God, for whom he was created. ('Declaration on Religious Freedom', n.3.)

Addressing the question in the 'Pastoral Constitution on the Church in the Modern World', Our Holy Father and the Bishops at the Second Vatican Council wrote:

In the depths of his conscience, man detects a law which he does not impose upon himself, but which holds him to obedience. Always summoning him to love good and avoid evil, the voice of conscience can when necessary speak to his heart more specifically: do this, shun that. For man has in his heart a law written by God. To obey it is the very dignity of man; according to it he will be judged.

Conscience is the most secret core and sanctuary of a man. There he is alone with God, whose voice echoes in his depths. In a wonderful way conscience reveals that law which is fulfilled by love of God and neighbour. In fidelity to conscience, Christians are joined with the rest of men in the search for truth, and for the genuine solution to the numerous problems which arise in the life of individuals and from social relationships.

Hence the more that a correct conscience holds sway, the more persons and groups turn aside from blind choice and strive to be guided by objective norms of morality. ('The Church in the Modern World', n.16.)

In addition, the Church has always affirmed the obligation of individuals to contribute to the common good and the general welfare of the larger community. This is the basis for the participation of Christians in the legitimate defence of their nation.

The Council Fathers, recognising the absence of adequate authority at the international level to resolve all disputes among nations, acknowledged that 'governments cannot be denied the right to legitimate defence once every means of peaceful settlement has been exhausted' ('The Church in the Modern World', n.79.)

When survival of the wider community has been threatened by external force, the Church has traditionally upheld the obligation of Christians to serve in military defensive forces. Such community-oriented service, that is, soldiers devoted to the authentic purposes of securing peace and justice, has merited the Church's commendation.

The Catholic Bishops of the United States are gratefully conscious of the sacrifices and valor of those men who are serving and who have served in the armed forces and especially those who have given their lives in service to their country. Their courage in the defence of the common good must not be underestimated or forgotten. In the words of the Second Vatican Council, 'As long as they (members of the armed forces) fulfill this role properly, they are making a genuine contribution to the establishment of peace'. ('The Church in the Modern World', n.79.)

It was also recognised by the Second Vatican Council that the common good is also served by the conscientious choice of those who renounce violence and war, choosing the means of nonviolence instead:

> . . . we cannot fail to praise those who renounce the use of violence in the vindication of their rights and who resort to methods of defence which are otherwise available to weaker parties too, provided that this can be done without injury to the rights and duties of others or of the community itself. ('The Church in the Modern World', n.78.)

Furthermore, the Council Fathers, addressing themselves more specifically to the rights of the conscientious objector to war, stated:

> . . . it seems right that laws make humane provisions for those who for reasons of conscience refuse to bear arms, provided however, that they accept some other form of service to the human community. ('The Church in the Modern World', n.79.)

Although a Catholic may take advantage of the law providing exemption from military service because of conscientious opposition to all war, there often arises a practical problem at the local level when those who exercise civil authority are of the opinion that a Catholic cannot under any circumstances be a conscientious objector because of religious training and belief. This confusion, in some cases, is the result of a mistaken notion that a person cannot be a conscientious objector unless the individual is a member of one of the traditional pacifist churches (for example, a Quaker).

In the light of the Gospel and from an analysis of the Church's teaching on conscience, it is clear that a Catholic can be a conscientious objector to war in general or to a particular war 'because of religious training and belief'. It is not enough, however, simply to declare that a Catholic can be a conscientious objector or a selective conscientious objector. Efforts must be made to help Catholics form a correct conscience in the matter, to discuss with them the duties of citizenship, and to provide them with adequate draft counselling and information services in order to give them the full advantage of the law protecting their rights. Catholic organisations which could qualify as alternative service agencies should be encouraged to support and provide meaningful employment for the conscientious objector. As we hold individuals in high esteem who conscientiously serve in the armed forces, so also we should regard conscientious objection and selective conscientious objection as positive indicators within the Church of a sound moral awareness and respect for human life.

The status of the selective conscientious objector is complicated by the fact that the present law does not provide an exemption for this type of conscientious objection. We recognise the very complex procedural problems which selective conscientious objection poses for the civil community; we call upon moralists, lawyers and civil servants to work co-operatively toward a policy which can reconcile the demands of the moral and civic order concerning this issue. We reaffirm the recommendation on this subject contained in our November 1968 pastoral letter, 'Human Life in Our Day':

> 1. a modification of the Selective Service Act making it possible for selective conscientious objectors to refuse to serve in wars they consider unjust, without fear of imprisonment or loss of citizenship, provided they perform some other service to the human community; and
> 2. an end to peacetime conscription.

In restating these recommendations, we are aware that a number of young men have left the country or have been imprisoned because of their opposition to compulsory military conscription. It is possible that in some cases this was done for unworthy motives, but in general we must presume sincere objections of conscience, especially on the part of those ready to suffer for their convictions. Since we have a pastoral concern for their welfare, we urge civil officials in revising the law to consider granting amnesty to those who have been imprisoned as selective conscientious objectors, and giving those who have emigrated an opportunity to return to the country to show responsibility for their conduct and to be ready to serve in other ways to show that they are sincere objectors.

Index

South African Army Non-Effective Troops Section (SAANETS), 65
South African Broadcasting Corporation (SABC), 30
South African Catholic Bishops' Conference (SACBC), 34, 46, 47, 70, 100
Administrative Board of, 34, 46
Report on Namibia, 102
South African Council of Churches (SACC), 14, 20, 28-35, 44-46, 52, 58, 62-63, 68, 73-75, 78
Council of Churches in Namibia, 21
Justice and Reconciliation Division, 46, 62
National Conference, 46, 68, 78
South African Defence Force (SADC), 7, 9, 15-16, 23, 33, 38, 42, 43, 49, 59, 61, 62, 64, 67, 68, 70-73, 94, 100, 102
Catholic Chaplains, 72
Chaplains' Corps, 67, 68
Chaplain General, 60, 67, 70, 73, 76
Citizen Force, 24, 66
Citizen Force and Commandos, 67
Defence Force bonds, 63
Medical Corps, 82
Paratus, 60, 61
Permanent Force, 43, 49, 67, 70
South African Broadcasting Corporation, 30
State Security Council (SSC), 18
Steele, Richard, 54, 56, 57, 83
Steyn Commission, 98

Storey, Rev. Peter, 35, 62, 63
SWAPO (South West African Peoples Organisation), 72, 94, 100, 102

TREURNICHT, Dr Andries, 18
Tutu, Bishop Desmond, 14, 21, 55

UCCSA (United Congregational Church of Southern Africa), 46, 48
General Assembly, 53
Umkhonto We Sizwe, 98
UNITA (National Union for the Total Independence of Angola), 37
United Board of Free Churches, 72
United Party, 29

VAN ZYL, Major-General J.A., 60, 67, 68
Vause Raw, W., 30
Verwoerd, Dr H.F., 59, 100
Vilonel, J.J., 82
Viveiros, Michael, 64, 65
Vorster, B.J., 24, 29
Vorster Koort, J.D., 31

WING, Rev. Joe, 46
Winter, Bishop Colin, 68
Women's Auxiliary, 70
World Reform Alliance, 9

YEATS Charles, 62, 64, 65

ZIONIST Church, 12
Zulu, Bishop Alphaeus, 13